LOVE
ACCEPTANCE
AND
FORGIVENESS

Being Christian in a
Non-Christian World

Jerry Cook *with*
Stanley C. Baldwin

Regal

From Gospel Light
Ventura, California, U.S.A.

Published by Regal
From Gospel Light
Ventura, California, U.S.A.
www.regalbooks.com
Printed in the U.S.A.

First Edition, 1979
Second Edition, 2009

Library of Congress Cataloging-in-Publication Data
The Library of Congress has cataloged the first edition as follows:
Cook, Jerry.
Love, acceptance & forgiveness / Jerry Cook, with Stanley C. Baldwin.
p. cm.
ISBN 978-0-8307-4753-5 (trade paper)
1. Theology, Practical. 2. Christian life.
BV3.C65
79063763

1 2 3 4 5 6 7 8 9 10 11 12 13 14 15 / 15 14 13 12 11 10 09

Rights for publishing this book outside the U.S.A. or in non-English languages
are administered by Gospel Light Worldwide, an international not-for-profit
ministry. For additional information, please visit www.glww.org, email
info@glww.org, or write to Gospel Light Worldwide, 1957 Eastman Avenue,
Ventura, CA 93003, U.S.A.

CONTENTS

PREFACE TO THE FIRST EDITION

The nature of Christ's church on this planet is of consuming interest to me not just because I am a pastor, but because I am also a part of that church. I came directly from seminary, and my wife from teaching to our tiny church of 23 people. We were equipped to answer all questions and forge into new streams of Christian thought, supposedly. We discovered we really knew nothing about our task. I had not come to grips with the nature of the true church of Christ.

We were driven by our congregation to face with them the implications of being truly Christian in a non-Christian and, at times, anti-Christian world. That adventure led us into the lives and homes of all *sorts* of people. We began to sense the thrill of the Jesus-life effectively invading and challenging every area of human hurt. From the confusion of the drug culture, to the violence of the street and motorcycle gangs, to the sophisticated offices of the executive set and everything in between, we saw the church function.

Suddenly, divorce was not merely a theological workshop but the heartbroken and disillusioned person sitting across the table. Drugs were not only a social evil but also the blank and tortured faraway look that makes a teenager suddenly an old person. We began to understand that the church was people—real people—changed by the power of Christ, filled with the Spirit of Christ, touching the hurting, dying and cynical modern man with the life of Jesus Himself.

"The church, which is His body, the fullness of Him . . ."

This book presents some of the viewpoints and perspectives we have learned together as a group of people serious about truly being His Body. It is written for the church—pastors, homemakers, taxi drivers, executives, blue collar, white collar or no collar. It is a sincere effort to share with you the sheer excitement that exists in being "the church."

I have found in Stan Baldwin a sensitive and perceptive writer. His questions, observations and balance have given to this book that which I alone could never have hoped to achieve. He has waded through hours of tapes and stacks of materials and has compiled those things we truly believe.

If in the reading of this you are called upon to question, evaluate or even change your thinking, so be it. What I desire is that all of us who go by the name "Christian" be effectively living out the implications of that name. It is time to get the church into the world and so fulfill the "Immanuel Principle"—God with us.

Jerry Cook, 1979

PREFACE TO
THE SECOND EDITION

The Harley roared past, pulled sharply in front of me, and then slowed down, daring me to pass. On the way by, the rider took a long, hard look into my window, slowing slightly, and then gunned on ahead. I pulled out to go around, and he matched my speed for a fraction, staring into the passenger's side window. He slowed down, let me pass, and then roared up on my bumper near the center line. He began motioning me to pull over.

Oregon is a beautiful state. It is divided into three very clear sections. There is the western section, bounded by the Pacific Ocean on the west and the Cascade Mountains on the east. The central section is bounded on the east by the same glorious snow-capped peaks of the Cascades, and then relaxes into a high desert that stretches into the eastern section and the Blue Mountains.

On this day, I was driving through a particularly empty section of Central Oregon to visit some friends. It was just me and this "biker," as we called the members of a few outlaw clubs in our area. The emblem and insignias, the hair, scars and tattoos all made it clear to me that he was not a weekend wonder.

I am no hero. My fight and flight response is heavily weighted toward the latter. My heart and breath rate indicated—FEAR! Yet as I began planning my escape, something inside of me said, *Pull over and talk to him.* My immediate response was, *Get behind me Satan!* I was not called by God to die at the hands of an outlaw biker on a deserted road in Central Oregon.

But the impression increased, and I found myself actually pulling off to the side of the road. *This is insane! What am I doing?* But he was off the bike and at my door (which I hadn't thought to lock). He opened the door and pulled me from my car to my certain death.

Suddenly, his arms were holding me in a huge, hairy embrace. Tears were running from his eyes into his ragged beard.

"You're Jerry Cook, ain't you?" he said.

"Who would like to know?" I sputtered.

The man began telling me a story. He had been a prisoner in a Washington federal prison, and the chaplain had given him a copy of *Love, Acceptance and Forgiveness*. He had read it and given his life to Christ. He experienced remarkable healing and change. He vowed that when he got out, he would look up this Jerry Cook who wrote the book, tell him the story and thank him.

He had come to our Sunday morning service the day before with the intention of seeing me. We were having several services at that time, and he couldn't manage to get through the crowd to the front where I was. Disappointed, he had decided to ride to Central Oregon to see some Christian brothers, where he recognized me on the road and gave me the most terrifying and excitingly wonderful experience of my life. As he was talking, I noticed that he did not have a skull or swastika hanging around his neck but a cross.

He and "the brothers" became the members of the first Christian bikers club on the West Coast. They were responsible for introducing literally hundreds—perhaps thousands, now—of their fellow bikers to Christ.

Love, Acceptance and Forgiveness was written more than 30 years ago out of the struggle and process of learning what it means to be the "Body of Christ" in our world. It wasn't the story of how churches grow; it was the story of how Jesus causes people to grow. We were not learning to do church well but were going through the painful, frustrating, confusing and wonderful process of being the church. These people weren't coming to church; they were *becoming* the church. Amazingly, that story has found its way into the most amazing places.

I am no longer a young pastor caught up in something truly divine. I have lived with these concepts for 30 years and have preached them all over the world and taught them in schools and seminaries. I have talked about these concepts over meals, on airplanes and in homes. I have lived long enough to see the dramatic and exciting effects that being Jesus in our world has on churches and individual believers. I am more deeply committed to this simple and yet profound concept now than ever before.

This book is not about technique. I care little about it. Methods are seldom transferable from one generation to another. The question must never be, *What are you doing?* but always, *Why are you doing this, and is it reproducing the life of Jesus in your world?* The "what" of today is very different than it was 30 years ago; it is even different than it was one year ago. The "why," however, always remains the same: to bring the transforming life of Jesus into our world . . . our world as it is today. There is no other assignment.

This new edition is an effort to speak into "our world as it is today." With a lot of help from people younger than I, we have fiddled with the language, updated some of the illustrations and expanded some subjects that are especially current now.

We have added a section for pastors and leaders and a guide to help you study it. But we have tried to keep the book essentially the same as it has been. God has remarkably blessed it and helped it be transferable into people's lives. It is our prayer that we have not tampered too much but simply given Him a further vehicle to continue His wonderful story of *Love, Acceptance and Forgiveness.*

Jerry Cook, 2009

A Place Where
People Are
Made Whole

A pastor in our town whom I knew only slightly became involved in adultery. As a result, his marriage went on the rocks and his ministry was destroyed. Because he was a strong Christian leader in our area, this pastor's fall came with a resounding crash. His church splintered into a dozen fragments and hurting, confused people were scattered all over the city.

A year and a half after all that happened, I received a phone call at 7:30 A.M. one Sunday. It was this former pastor. He said, "Would you mind if my wife and I came to East Hill Church this morning?"

I said, "Why would you even call and ask that question? Of course we wouldn't mind."

"Well," he said, "you know this is my second wife and I am divorced from my first. Are you aware of this?"

I said, "Sure, I'm aware of it."

"Well," he said, "I'll tell you, Jerry, we've been trying for eight months now to find a place to worship. The last time we tried was a month ago. That morning, we were asked from the pulpit to leave. We've been met at the door of other churches by pastors who heard that my wife and I were coming. They asked us not to come in; they said we would cause too much trouble. Still others have heard that we might show up and called in advance to ask us please not to come. Frankly, I don't think we could handle it again if we were to come and be an embarrassment to you and be asked to leave. I just don't know what would happen; my wife is close to a nervous breakdown."

By now he was weeping. "I know that you have video for overflow crowds," he said. "If you want, you can put us in a room where no one will see us and let us watch the service."

"Listen," I said. "You be there, and I'll welcome you at the door."

He came with his wife and their little baby. They arrived late and sat in the back.

What compounded the situation was that many of the people who had been hurt through his fall were now a part of our congregation. Nevertheless, we extended an open door to that couple, and the Lord did a cleansing and a healing. We shed so many tears together. I will never forget how he grabbed me and buried his head on my shoulder, a man 15 to 20 years my senior. He wept like a baby and held on to me like a drowning man. He said, "Jerry, can you love me? I've spent my life loving people, but I need someone to love me now."

In the weeks and months that followed, he met with some of our trusted leaders regularly and wept his way back to God through a most intense and sometimes utterly tearing repentance. If ever in my entire life I've seen godly sorrow for sin, I saw it in that man. He literally fell on the floor, grabbed our feet and implored us, "Can you ever forgive me?"

God healed him and restored him to wholeness. His second marriage, born in chaos, was salvaged—and all because God enabled us to love him, accept him and forgive him. Love, acceptance, forgiveness—those three things are absolutely essential to consistently bring people to maturity and wholeness. If the church—the living presence of Christ in His people—is to be the force for God in the world that it should be, it must learn to love people, accept them and forgive them.

Jesus said, "The Son of Man came to seek and to save what was lost" (Luke 19:10). The word "save" or "salvation" in its broadest sense means to bring to wholeness. It's interchangeable with the word "healing." In James 5:15 we read, "And the prayer of faith shall save the sick" (*KJV*). The same Greek word rendered "save" in this verse is translated "heal" elsewhere. For instance, the *NIV* says, "And the prayer offered in faith will make the sick person well."

People need to be saved and brought to wholeness in every area of their lives. But before there can be a coming to wholeness, certain guarantees must be made to them. Otherwise, they will not risk opening themselves to us enough to receive healing.

The minimal guarantee we must make is that we will love them—always, under every circumstance, with no exceptions. The second guarantee is that we will accept them totally, without reservation. The third thing we must guarantee people is that no matter how miserably they fail or how blatantly they sin, our unreserved forgiveness is theirs for the asking with no bitter taste left in anybody's mouth.

If people are not guaranteed these three things, they will never allow us the marvelous privilege of bringing wholeness to them through the fellowship of the church.

I will develop these concepts more fully later, but for now remember that there are three statements we must always keep in mind when dealing with these ideas: (1) love is not license, (2) acceptance is not agreement, and (3) forgiveness is not compromise.

Love One Another

"We know that we have passed from death to life, because we love our brothers. Anyone who does not love remains in death" (1 John 3:14). According to this Scripture, the evidence that we're children of God is our love for other believers. If love is lacking in our lives, we "remain in death." We are not the sons and daughters of God, no matter what experience we claim in the past.

Now, for me that is both frightening and liberating. How do I know that I have passed from death unto life? Well, there was that time I got down on my knees . . . or said a prayer . . . and that time when I was confirmed or baptized . . . but no, that's not good enough. I know I'm a child of God because I love others. That's not some theological or philosophical statement. I actually do love others, and that is evidence of God's Spirit living in me. You see, in the natural, I don't love anybody. My personal history is one of exploitation and manipulation of other people. But now I love them. Therefore, I know I that am a child of God, because my daily experience verifies it.

Today, those of us in the church of Jesus Christ need to make a bold commitment to love people and then dedicate ourselves to fulfilling that commitment. Our whole lifestyle should tell people, "If you come around here, we're going to love you. No matter who you are, what you've done or how you look, smell or behave, we're going to love you."

We must remember that the word for love here is *agape*. *Agape* love first exists, and then it affects the emotions. "For God so loved the world that He sat in heaven and had warm feelings?" No, that's nonsense. "For God so loved the world that He gave" (John 3:16). That's it! *Agape* is a volitional commitment to another that motivates us to act on his or her behalf. Every time we find a corresponding action to the concept of *agape*, it is a giving action.

There is no doubt that strong and appropriate emotions often actualize loving behavior. In Scripture, we read that Jesus was moved with compassion (see Matt. 9:36; 14:14; 20:34). But we must never confuse a shallow sensation that may inspire an impulsive response as love. Compassion, understanding, identification, gratitude, empathy, gentleness and appreciation are some of the heartfelt experiences that may accompany our loving behavior.

Furthermore, *agape* involves the kind of giving that cannot be compensated. That concept of love is quite foreign to our culture. The mentality of this world leads us to love and give only when there is reason to assume that our love will be reciprocated. This reciprocity is tested carefully during a "getting acquainted" time. If things look promising, and if our approach is met with acceptance and response, we risk a bit further, and a friendship is established. We first get acquainted and then move into love . . . sometimes. As a result, most people have many acquaintances and a few friends, but they are dying from lack of love.

In the kingdom of God, we first love and then move into acquaintance. Love is a commitment and operates independently of what we feel or do not feel. We need to extend this love to everyone: "I want you to know that I'm committed to you. You'll never knowingly suffer at my hands. I'll never say or do anything, knowingly, to hurt you. I'll always in every circumstance seek to help you and support you. If you're down and I can lift you up, I'll do that. Anything I have that you need, I'll share with you; and if need be, I'll give it to you. No matter what I find out about you and no matter what happens in the future, either good or bad, my commitment to you will never change. And there's nothing you can do about it. You don't have to respond. I love you, and that's what it means."

When we can make that commitment to every person, our church community will begin to be one that's learning to love and be a force for God.

Sometimes when I am teaching, I select an individual from the group whom I do not know. I express the forever love commitment to him or her personally before everyone. I do it for effect, but it is also my sincere commitment to that person. One of these people came to me several years later and reminded me of the commitment I had made to him. In fact, he repeated it to me almost word for word. "I've been up all night in anticipation of talking to you," he said. "I have to tell you that I've blown it." He then proceeded to describe the chaos in his life, his marriage and his ministry.

As his shocking story unfolded, I found myself becoming angry and disgusted with him for insulting the name of Jesus and forfeiting his ministry so foolishly. *Dear God*, I thought, *what have I gotten myself into? Can I really keep my commitment to this man? When he's all done pouring himself out to me, can I totally accept him and not think any less of him?* I was not at all sure that I could.

But while he was speaking, a strange thing happened. I sensed real compassion for the man. When he was through, I said to him, "What you have told me is probably the most disgusting, despicable thing I can think of. I don't know of anything more you could have done to destroy your life and self-respect. You've left no stone unturned. But you need to know that as you were talking, the Holy Spirit gave me a deep love for you. And because I love you and that love has been placed in my heart by the Holy Spirit, God loves you and offers you complete forgiveness."

The way the man began to weep, it was like turning on a faucet. Then he prayed. On the basis of my love, he asked God to forgive him. The outworking of all that over a period of time brought about the restoration of his home and his life, and now he is serving Christ.

This man had to tell someone. And because I had made that commitment to him, he felt he could come to me. He was at a point emotionally where he could not risk rejection, but neither could he keep silent. Like many other hurting people, he desperately needed someone to love him, and he had almost nowhere to turn.

Love Is Not License

Our love for others must never be confused as a license for their destructive behavior toward us, toward others or toward themselves. Love commits itself to their "highest good" and stands stubbornly and relentlessly against their destruction from any quarter.

My wife, Barbara, was the pastor of a large group of college students and young single professionals. One day, a young woman came to her and shared some deep regrets.

"As a young teenager, I was so mean and hateful to Mom." she said. "I swore at her and called her horrible names. I even yelled 'I hate you' at her many times during my selfish little temper tantrums."

"What did your mother do?" Barb asked.

"Nothing. She just took it."

"What do you think she should have done?"

"She should have done anything she had to do to stop me—even slap my dirty mouth!"

"How did talking like that cause you to feel about her?" Barb said.

"I actually started to believe she deserved it. I was so destructive. I began to hate her and hate myself, too."

"Did she ever tell you why she didn't stop you?"

"Because she was afraid I would think she didn't love me. I think the most loving thing she could have done would have been to stop me."

Whether it is an intervention into an addiction or refusing to enable abusive or rebellious behavior in a child or friend, love always steps in the way of destructive behavior. Not to do so is an act of hatred, not love.

A young doctor commented on this love lifestyle: "Our lifestyle expresses not only love but also what we will tolerate and not tolerate in a relationship. There needs to be absolute love but a zero tolerance for destructive behavior in the relationship."

Acceptance: The Gift of Significance

I took a year's break between my second and third year of seminary, when our first daughter was born. I worked at a steel warehouse loading and unloading trucks and train cars full of steel. I often worked with a fellow who had one of the filthiest mouths I've ever heard on a human being. I've been in the Army and worked on construction sites where the language turned the air various shades of blue, but Charlie was in a class all his own. He literally could not finish a sentence without vomiting filth everywhere.

For some reason, Charlie took a liking to me. He decided he was going to be my friend and curse and swear me right through the day. We'd load trucks together and—oh man!—not only did he swear a lot, but he also talked a lot. He talked constantly, even when there was nothing to say, and then he'd seal it with a curse.

In time, I came to like Charlie. He was a unique character, and he had a great sense of humor. We'd eat lunch together, and he would swear me through lunch. This went on for three or four months. Then one day as we were eating lunch, he said to me, "Boy, my wife sure likes you."

I didn't know what to make of his comment. Coming from him, it could mean anything.

"Charlie, I don't believe that I've ever met your wife," I answered.

"No, no, you never have, but she sure likes you."

"Well, you're going to have to help me out here," I said.

"She told me the other day that since I've been working with you, I've been swearing less."

"Really? I hadn't noticed!"

"Yeah, it's true."

"I didn't know that you wanted to swear less," I told him. "I thought you talked the way you wanted to."

Charlie stopped cold and looked at me soberly. "Jerry, I have tried to stop swearing all my life," he said. "I was raised in a home where I learned swear words before I learned English. I can't remember ever hearing anything else until I started going to school. It's the only way I've ever talked. I'm so embarrassed by the way I talk. I don't go out to dinner or anyplace else, because I know I offend people. But since I've been hanging out with you, I've been talking better, and that's encouraging to me and my wife."

Before I left that job, I had a wonderful chance to pray with Charlie, and we became even better friends.

Love means accepting people the way they are for Jesus' sake. Jesus hung around with sinners. He didn't isolate Himself in the synagogue. In fact, Jesus mixed with sinners so much that the self-righteous people got upset about it. "He's friendly with some very questionable people," they said. And Jesus replied, "Yes, because I didn't come to minister to you religious leaders. I came to call sinners to repentance."

Isn't that fantastic? Jesus spent His time with dirty, filthy, stinking, bent sinners. And when those kinds of people find someone who will love and accept them, you won't be able to keep them away.

A young man phoned me early one morning and said, "I'm going to commit suicide."

I said, "Why are you talking to me?"

He said, "Because I don't want to do it, but I don't know what else to do. I'm a heroin addict, and last night I nearly killed a man." He told me the circumstances, how he'd been stopped from killing this man. He said, "I'm afraid to go home. I'm afraid to do anything. I'm totally out of control, and the only thing I know to do is end my life."

I asked him if we could get together. "No way," he said. "I called a pastor a few months ago and he told me to come by his office. When I got there, he had the sheriff waiting to pick me up. I spent the next six months in jail. I made up my mind then that I wasn't about to go to another preacher."

My heart broke. What could I do? I said, "Look, I'll go to my office right now. Give me 15 minutes. Then you drive by the church until you're satisfied that no one else is around. I'll stay there for three hours. If at any time during those three hours you want to risk coming in, I'll be the only one there."

I waited at the church for two and a half hours. Finally, I heard the front door open, and then a knock on my office door. I let him in. He gave his life to Christ right there. It was a powerful, beautiful kind of thing. The heart-breaking question is why this man hadn't found love and acceptance before in the one place on earth that's supposed to know how to love. Pastors and congregations who are afraid of green hair, piercings and tattoos are in the wrong business.

"But what will sister-so-and-so think?"

Does it really matter? The church should state, "We're going to love and accept people, and if you don't want to love people, you're in the wrong place. This church is going to love people." Unreserved acceptance of people should be a habit with us. There's no other way to get close enough to people to help them at the level of their deepest needs. When we cultivate the habit of accepting people, they open up to us, they like us, and they trust us instinctively.

I was at the county courthouse getting a passport one day when I spotted a young couple I recognized as being from our church. I asked what they were doing there and discovered that they were getting a marriage license. "Well, Pastor," the young man said, "we've been living together for about four years now, and we figured we might as well do it right. Say, I forgot to bring anyone along. Would you mind being a witness for us?"

Now, this young man did not have a particularly soft voice, and there were about 25 people in that office. For some reason, the whole room suddenly became very quiet. I felt that every eye in the place was on me, a pastor who had just been identified as knowing a young couple who were living together and not married. What was I to do? Say to the fellow, "Shh-shh, don't let anybody hear you"? Or give a little sermon of rebuke just so everyone would know that I disapproved?

"Hey, that's fantastic," I said. "You're getting married!" And I signed as a witness.

I accepted that couple. There was no question as to whether I agreed with their lifestyle. They knew I didn't. However, I had accepted them long before this encounter, and my acceptance was so solid that they weren't afraid to tell me the truth now. I praise the Lord for that, because I can remember a day when a person in their situation seeing me in there would have slipped away and come back only after I was gone.

Because we are accepted in the Beloved, we must be accepting of the beloved. We can't give up on others until God does—and He won't! We're safe with God, and we've got to be safe with one another. We've got to be able to know that we can blow it and still be loved.

I know that I'm only human. In fact, you have no idea how human I am. You little realize the weakness and the frailty of the man who lives in this frame. But I know, and I contend with it every day. I'm just mud, as you are. I've got to be able to fail and still be loved and accepted—by my wife, by my children, by my congregation, by my close friends. I simply cannot live with rejection by those I love and value. That's not because I'm on an ego trip, but because I'm a person.

Acceptance Is Not Agreement

Earlier, I told about a fallen pastor who was restored to fellowship because he found love, acceptance and forgiveness at East Hill. What I did not tell you is that a barrage of phone calls began coming to us shortly after that time from irate pastors and other people. They were terribly upset that our accepting him would be interpreted as license for what he had done. I suppose that is possible. Perhaps some people would be so blind. But they would be wrong to make that assumption. We were neither countenancing his sin nor trying to be noble and heroic in bucking the tide of sentiment against him. We were simply and plainly loving him.

A leading church official called me during this time. He asked, "Do you know what you've done?"

I assured him that I most likely did not.

"Well," he said, "you've opened your doors to every broken-down pastor with ethical problems there is."

My answer to that was, "Praise the Lord. If they can't come here, where can they go? Where do we refer them? If people can't be healed in our congregation, where should we send them? Someone has to be the end of the line for messed-up humanity. We are not in a popularity contest."

Jesus was crucified at the end of His ministry, and it was the equivalent of the local ministerial association that put Him on the cross. The religious community may put us on the cross, too. If so, pray that God will forgive them. The very ones who would crucify us may also fall some day, and when they do, they should be able to come to us and find love, acceptance and forgiveness. They should find a welcome and hear a voice saying, "Friend, I know you are hurting. In Jesus' name, come in."

Never labor under the misconception that such acceptance will breed license. To the contrary, our very acceptance of others can make them strong. It will never confuse them in questions of right and wrong if our teaching and personal lifestyle establish clear standards. For example, a person who is caught up in a lesbian or homosexual lifestyle will not assume that because we value him or her as a person, we agree with their lifestyle. Acceptance is not based on approved behavior. It is based on the value of the person. But if we communicate personal rejection, they will never be around long enough to be touched by God through us.

The same principle applies in all our relationships with other people. Jesus accepts us even though we have much in our lives that offends His holiness. His acceptance of us does not imply His approval of our destructive behavior. If, then, we are acceptable to Jesus, who do we think we are to reject others?

Forgiveness: Refusing to Play God

"Be kind and compassionate to one another, forgiving each other, just as in Christ God forgave you" (Eph. 4:32).

I like Catherine Marshall's concept of forgiveness that she develops in her book *Something More*. She suggests that forgiveness is releasing another from our own personal judgment. Taking our personal judgment off a person doesn't mean that we agree with what he has said or done; it simply means that we will not act as his or her judge. We will not pronounce a guilty verdict on that person.

"But he was wrong," you say.

Okay, but he's not standing under your judgment. You release him.

To keep others under our personal judgment is to play God with them. Romans 12:19 says, " 'It is mine to avenge; I will repay,' says the Lord." And because He's going to repay, we don't have to.

"But that person hurt me, Lord. Did You know that?"

"Of course."

"Well, are You going to do anything about it?"

"What do you think?"

"Are You going to strike him dead?"

"Probably not."

"But, Lord . . ."

"Do you want to play God? If so, remember this: The moment you step in to bring judgment onto that person, you will come under My judgment."

"Do not judge, and you will not be judged. . . . Forgive, and you'll be forgiven" (Luke 6:37). Release people from your personal judgment! For unless they can be assured of your forgiveness, they cannot really open themselves to you. You see, sooner or later, people will disappoint you and fail you. Not by design or desire, but because they are imperfect. They must know that you will not condemn them when their weaknesses, flaws and sins begin to show. They need the assurance of your forgiveness—a forgiveness with no bitter aftertaste.

Forgiveness is simply the choice not to punish, but it gets tangled up with all sorts of other ideas and becomes almost scary. Here are some myths we struggle with:

- *"Forgive and forget."* Try pulling that off sometime and let me know if you succeed!

- *When you forgive, you will feel better.* There are events so painful in your life that whenever you remember them you will always sense the hurt. How you feel after you forgive is irrelevant. You may feel better, or you may feel nothing. The issue is not how you feel; it is whether you intend to keep punishing and getting even with the person.

- *Forgiveness means that you must move back into a destructive relationship.* The fact is that there are people with whom you may never be able to have a healthy relationship. Some people are so damaged emotionally and socially that they are not capable of sustaining a healthy relationship with anyone. Forgiveness can provide a basis for re-establishing a healthy relationship, but it doesn't demand the re-establishment of an unhealthy one.

• *If you forgive, you are compromising or condoning wrong behavior.* Forgiveness doesn't deal with guilt or innocence. Justice deals with guilt and innocence. You forgiving someone else doesn't mean that what he or she did was okay. What he or she did may never be okay in anybody's book.

Ultimately, forgiveness is not an emotion; it's a *decision*. We don't forgive with our memory or emotions—we forgive with our will. It's a choice we make not to enter into a lifestyle of revenge and punishment, of getting even. This reduces things to such simplicity. It frees us up to love one another and not have to worry about being each other's guardians. It allows pastors to not be wardens of the flock but shepherds of the flock. There's a big difference, and it's the difference between loving and judging.

When love, acceptance and forgiveness characterize our lives and our churches, the Lord will send us people who need to be made whole. A pastor friend called me one day very upset. He was irritated because some of his people had started coming to our church. I knew what he was talking about and felt he needed to get it off his chest, so I let him talk. At one point he said, "You know what you are out there? You're nothing but a bunch of garbage collectors."

As I thought about it, I realized he was telling the truth. That's exactly what we were: garbage collectors. What were we before Jesus found us? Weren't we all just garbage? Jesus finds us and recycles us.

I mentioned this in church one Sunday, and afterward a man who owned a garbage collection agency came charging up the aisle, all excited. "That's incredible," he said. "Let me tell you something about garbage. There's a landfill near here. For 10 years, we used it as a place to dump trash and garbage. Know what's there now? A beautiful park."

I've seen human garbage become beautiful too. I've seen the stench of sin turned into the fragrance of heaven. That's our business. We can't worry about what critics think or say. Where is God going to send the "garbage" for recycling? If He can't put it on our doorstep, or if we are not open for business, someone else will be. And we will lose a great opportunity to bring healing in a hurting person's life.

When love, acceptance and forgiveness prevail, the church of Jesus Christ becomes what Jesus was in the world: a center of love designed for the healing of broken people and a force for God.

The Need for a Guiding Philosophy

One thing working all kinds of devastation in the life of the church is the failure of the leadership to have a solid philosophy—a well-defined concept of how a church ought to operate and why. In the absence of such a philosophy, pastors tend to do one of the following: (1) they pastor from crisis to crisis, (2) they pick up on the current fad, or (3) they simply subscribe to a concept of church life handed down to them.

Crisis to Crisis

A great deal of a pastor's life can be spent rushing from crisis to crisis so that he or she never has the opportunity to sit down and think through the question, *What in the world am I really in existence for anyway?*

It's easy to be trapped by the pressure of a moment. Pastors find themselves thrown into situations, and they have to deal with what's there. Problems arise in the personal lives of their people. Someone passes away, for instance, so the pastor quickly prepares a sermon about death. Or maybe there has been a major accident. The people involved were

Christians, so questions arise about the sovereignty of God. So the pastor quickly works up a message on the sovereignty of God.

Problems arise in the groups that comprise each congregation. Maybe one of the girls in the youth group becomes pregnant, an unwed mother-to-be. Parents are upset, and the kids are asking questions. The result is a crisis in the youth department, and the pastor must step in and respond to the situation.

Next, there's trouble with the church board. The church is buying property. Suddenly, it becomes apparent that the congregation is party to a totally inadequate contract. The church is overcommitted and underfinanced. Now the pastor must run to that crisis.

Problems arise in performing the pastoral duties themselves. *Oh, boy, here it is Friday evening already, and I've hardly started to prepare my Sunday morning message. What in the world am I going to do?* It's another crisis.

Stop! Ask one question: Are pastors to spend their entire lives on call as a spiritual ambulance, or is there something more fundamental they should be doing?

One basic premise in my own philosophy of the church is that the people themselves are the ministers. Sunday morning is a meeting of the church staff. When a crisis arises, it doesn't necessarily have to come to the pastor's office. When someone passes away (to stick with a foregoing example), the situation does not call for a theological treatise. It calls for people who understand the nature of grief and bereavement to move in and, in a servant way, meet the personal needs of the sorrowing.

It is not the pastor's job to meet everybody's need. It is the pastor's job to see that everybody's need is met. That is the difference between facilitating ministry and just running an ambulance service. The pastor should be a facilitator.

But we must have a basic health plan underlying all this, and that's where the pastor needs to be coming from. Two things are necessary for this to occur: (1) people must be trained to use their own gifts in ministry, and (2) the church must grant the people the right to minister in crisis situations on the spot.

Crises cannot be avoided. They cannot even be scheduled. When a marriage blows up, someone's heart is breaking and the whole situation is about to go up in smoke, we can't say, "Well, let's see now, the pastor can see you a week from next Tuesday at 4:00 P.M." But we can involve people in ministry to the point that needs are met and the pastor is free of a constant demand to intervene in crises.

Church Fads

In the past few years, we in the church have run the gamut on fads. We've struggled to be seeker-sensitive. We've changed from organs and pianos to worship bands. We've downloaded and uploaded. We've changed services to Saturday night; we've shortened our services; we've programmed our gatherings for TV. We've found ourselves in a competitive supermarket of church programs and exhausted ourselves, our finances and our congregations trying to respond to a consumer mentality. Families shop and hop from one place to the next as we frantically look for what works.

Of course, we have to be progressive and respond to our changing culture. But too often we are only asking "what" questions and not "why" questions. We ask, "What will get more people into our building? What program will recruit and militate our volunteers? What new small-group scheme can we enact?"

I'm not saying that we should scrap small groups, do away with volunteers and go back to organs. I am just saying that we should stop a minute and ask, "What is our overall philosophy? Why are we doing small groups? Where does it fit in our philosophy? Are we disrupting the natural groupings among our people? Do we really need to order their social life and determine who their friends should be? Are we demanding so much of their time in Christian groups that they have no time to pursue other friendships and relationships outside the church community? Are we unknowingly introducing conflicting demands?"

As I have taught these concepts in every conceivable setting and location for the past 30 years, I have been troubled at the number of church leaders who change their semantic to marketplace ministry and "being Jesus in our world," but then continue to introduce complex, time-consuming programs that necessitate a huge staff and block the people from actually living out what they are talking about. The congregation is solicited for every kind of volunteerism, which takes large chunks out of their already busy lives.

Musicians show up one or sometimes two nights each week (not including what happens at Christmas and Easter) to spend hours practicing songs they have known and played for years—or new songs they have never heard and the congregation can't sing and doesn't like. Or, like the church I mentioned earlier, meetings at the church building multiply: ushers' meetings, teachers' meetings, board meetings, men's meetings, women's meetings, leaders' meetings, committee meetings of every description. Because many of the same people are involved in one or all of these, every night of the week is soon taken up in some kind of "church work." Too often, a frequent and generous amount of guilt is added to the process through phrases like, "If you really are serious about serving God and your church, you will . . ." "God hates a lazy Christian," and other well-turned manipulative comments.

People's gifts are assessed, and they are assigned appropriate placement in maintaining the church structure, all in the name of serving God. People become disillusioned, to say nothing of exhausted. They no longer even have time for their families, let alone developing meaningful friendships with unbelievers, neighbors and associates.

The only way for us to get our walk aligned with our talk is to have a clear, guiding philosophy. Our culture is incredibly fractured. The generation gap has dramatically widened. Class distinction is raising its ugly head, and suspicion divides us. People shoot each other on highways, in shopping malls, in schools and in the workplace. They're stressed out and take pills for their stress disorders, and then their kids steal them and become addicted. Everyone is vying for rights: gay rights, worker rights, patient rights, children's rights, spousal rights, client rights, animal rights. It seems to keep expanding. The rush to rights at the very least means that we are becoming more greedy, selfish and uncaring. We have to wrest our rights through politics rather than relationships.

It is the church of Jesus Christ that should stand as a model of right in a sea of wrong. As the Bible puts it, we need to be light in a dark place (see Matt. 5:14). Does the way we do church provide these models clearly in our unbelieving culture? Too often we are isolated, alienated and looked at with suspicion by the very ones with whom we need to be connecting. We should not be as concerned about being "relevant" as being prophetic. This means that we should be speaking what God is speaking. The gift of prophecy is a gift of insight. We should be bringing God's insight into situations.

What if Jesus were living in our country now? How would He deal with the cultural pressures we face? He said, "As the Father speaks, I speak. I simply see what the Father is doing and I do it" (see John 5:19). That is being prophetic. We must begin to see what Christ is seeing and respond accordingly. He didn't start a political movement; in fact, He shunned politics. Yet He was involved politically, not from a movement point of view, but because what He did had fantastic political implications.

The prophetic lifestyle is person-oriented. For instance, to deal with homosexuality in an alienating way would be to deal with the issue of gay rights. I'm not primarily concerned about that as an issue, but I am concerned with a person who is caught in a lifestyle and who is being led to believe that he or she can never change. The truth is that he or she can change and that Jesus wants him or her to change. A host of people who have changed proves it can be done.

If we are to live prophetically, we must get to the individual. Making public statements won't accomplish the task—that only provides an occasion for others to voice an alternate viewpoint, and soon all we're doing is firing back and forth at each other. I don't think the church should get into that kind of conflict. To live prophetically in the world means to speak Christ's love and redemptive power into the heart of the individuals caught in sin. We see Jesus doing this. He didn't speak generally to the world, but He did confront individuals—He touched this sick person, He released that demon-possessed person, He forgave the other person who was a notorious sinner.

There is great concern today about church growth and establishing new congregations through church planting. We seem to be in a time in which people are rushing to get something—anything—started. But true church growth does not basically depend on methodology. The dynamic for church growth is Spirit-filled people meeting other people's needs in Jesus' name wherever they are. You can't reduce that to methodology.

I am not convinced that doing church the way we are in the Western world is particularly successful. In the United States, we have bigger churches than we have ever had, but we are a more secular society than we have ever been. I'm not laying the secularization of America on the doorstep of the church, but it does indicate that we are not penetrating our culture to any great extent. I don't know why doing more of what isn't particularly effective is so important. Furthermore, I don't read anyplace in Scripture where we are asked to plant churches. We are asked to "go and make disciples" (Matt. 28:19). Jesus said, "I will build my church" (Matt. 16:18). I don't read anywhere where He delegated that job to us.

I believe in planting *people*. Jesus certainly calls people to specific places. It's rather exciting to come to a community with the sole object of being Jesus and serving. Jesus may decide to build a church, and if He does, "The gates of hell shall not prevail against it" (Matt. 16:18, *KJV*).

Traditional Ways

Those of us who belong to a denomination, particularly a denomination with many years of history and well-developed worship traditions, are likely to subscribe to a concept of church life that was simply handed down to us.

If we are isolated from others, living within the context of monologue so far as church life goes, we will probably accept uncritically many practices that have no validity. Or, if they are valid, we don't know why and therefore cannot use them to best advantage. And we are totally unaware of alternatives that might suit our particular situation much better. A superficial exposure to new forms won't do any good either. What's needed is a change in the basic pattern of being bound by tradition.

Unless we want to be aggressive—unless we want to be current in the true sense of the word—we can use "in" terms such as "fellowship" or "marketplace" or "being Jesus in the world" and simply inject them into our existing traditional flow. We are not changing at all. We are only superimposing new semantics on old patterns of operation. We must always ask, "What is the application of church life out in the street? How can what we are doing inside affect life out there? Is worship an event that takes place, or is it a lifestyle?"

The beginning point for developing a philosophy is to really want to know where we are going and to have the courage to do some basic self-evaluation. People often see worship as a means to an end. But I don't believe worship is a means; it is an accomplishment in itself. The Father is seeking people who will worship Him in spirit and in truth.

People see sermons as vehicular. The preacher is going to say some things so that at the end he can insert a hook and draw people in the direction he wants them to go—to salvation, to commitment, to support of the building program, to start family worship or whatever. The sermon becomes a vehicle to get the hook in the fish. I don't view preaching that way. The Bible says we speak as the oracles of God (see 1 Pet. 4:11), which means that speaking itself is ministry. Preaching is to be oracular, not vehicular. As Jesus put it, "The words I have spoken to you are spirit and they are life" (John 6:63).

Speaking as an oracle of God means that the speaking in and of itself is used by the Spirit to accomplish ministry. As a pastor speaks, people should be saved, changed and encouraged. That was how it worked with Peter. "While Peter was still speaking these words, the Holy Spirit came on all who heard the message" (Acts 10:44). It worked this way with Jesus, too. As He spoke, people were healed and changed. When He finished speaking, there was no need to hang around and pray. The work was done.

What I am saying is that we should not see valid forms of ministry as vehicles to something else. The preaching of the Word is a powerful form of ministry. When God speaks through us, His word is life and brings life. We are not just downloading a sermon that suits the way we want the congregation to respond. We don't just go to www.illustrations.com and grab a good story. We don't go into some trance or become hyper. We get into the Word and let it speak to us, and then we speak the very words of God. It is far more important that our hearers hear what the Bible has said to us rather than what we are saying about the Bible. That is the force of true biblical preaching.

Music in the services is also often seen strictly as a vehicle. We have a worship band, which sets the mood for the sermon, which sets the mood for the hook. We do all this setting of the mood. No wonder when our people hit the marketplace it's inconceivable to them that they could say five words and strike the heart of a person with a direct message from God. They think the "prospect" has to be set up first. Not only does very little happen in the marketplace because of such thinking but, also, despite all this fantastic setting-up in the church services, nothing much happens there either. What we should seek is valid ministry in each component that comprises the meeting. During worship, something should be happening among the people. "All of these must be done for the strengthening of the church" (1 Cor. 14:26).

Nothing I have said about the dangers of traditional forms should be understood to imply that form is unimportant or undesirable. In the Old Testament, it was only after everything was finished in minute detail according to the prescribed pattern that the glory of God came into the Tabernacle (see Exod. 40:34). It is inconceivable to me that form should be thrown out and that everything should be totally unstructured. We need some kind of form in which to operate. Our whole life needs to be orderly. Form gives order to what we do. What I'm saying is that we shouldn't *worship* the form or be held captive to certain styles or methods.

Principles, Not Specifics

Every church needs a solid philosophical base upon which to build its life and ministry. I will outline such a philosophy in the next chapter, but remember that we will be talking about basic principles and not about specific practices as such. The principles, if they are sound, will work for anyone anywhere. The practices, on the other hand, relate to my specific situation, my community, my personality. Chances are they will not work well for you in your situation.

For example, I don't stand behind a pulpit when I preach. I usually sit on a stool. No great principle is at stake here, I just began the practice of sitting while preaching because my legs would get tired. I did not, however, break with the pulpit tradition easily. I had always stood behind a pulpit, and it had never even occurred to me that there might be an alternative. But my legs began to protest. I found myself preaching five times a Sunday and unable even to straighten my legs when it came time to get out of bed on Monday morning.

Finally, one of the young men in my congregation said, "Why don't you sit down while you preach?" I had never heard of that before. It sounded totally irreligious. Then he showed me from Scripture that Jesus sat and taught the people (see Matt. 26:55). "If Jesus could sit down and teach," he said, "you should be able to as well. Your sermons aren't quite as good, but otherwise it would be okay."

The next Sunday, I sat on an old wooden kitchen stool. It felt so good to get off my feet. More than that, though, sitting down broke me loose from the grip of tradition, and it unfettered the congregation as well. It got us moving in some very interesting directions. I have gotten quite used to sitting while I preach now. I tell audiences that if they feel someone should be standing while I preach, they can go ahead and stand.

But sitting while you preach is a specific practice, not a principle. I received a letter one day from a man who had attended a pastor's conference at which I had spoken. He said that when he went home, he got rid of their songbooks. He threw out the pulpit. He brought in a stool to sit on while he preached. Then he said, "And brother, there's still nothing happening here!"

Nothing will happen just because we make some practices a fad. But things will happen when we put the Bible's principles into practice. We will search out some of those principles next.

THE CHURCH
AS A FORCE

A mother was distraught because her two little boys were be-having badly and traumatizing their whole neighborhood. One day, the mother went next door and began pouring out her woes to her neighbor. The neighbor offered a solution. She once had a similar problem with her little boy. She took him to a nearby Catholic church and made him confess to the priest. That took care of the problem.

The distraught mother decided to do the same thing. She marched her boys down to the Catholic church and turned them over to the priest. The priest took the first boy aside and said, "Young man, where is God?"

The little boy was petrified and didn't answer. So the priest repeated the question. The little boy jumped up, ran from the priest, grabbed his brother and said, "We've got to get out of here. They've lost God, and they're trying to pin it on us."

Communication is a very interesting thing. I may know exactly what I'm going to say but still not have the faintest idea what you're going to hear. That is one reason why I want to relieve you right now of ever having to agree with me. Besides that, I don't speak as an authority. I'm simply a person trying to apply the significance of the Christian life and lifestyle in the arena where Jesus Christ has placed me.

With that in mind, let me ask you two questions: *What is the church?* and, *Where is the church?* You may not fully understand what I am going to say about the church. You may understand well enough but disagree with me. That is your privilege. But whether you like *my* answers or not, you should have well-thought-out answers to those questions.

I'm sure that thousands of Christian people have no satisfactory answer. Neither do many pastors. I've talked with pastors all over this nation who have absolutely no concept of what the church is. They've never thought about it. Oh, they studied the subject in a class in college or seminary. They have a notebook someplace, and they accept the definition in the notebook, but they aren't quite sure what that is or what it implies.

Then they begin to walk into people's lives, handling crisis after crisis, hiring staff, forming organizations, building structures and accumulating money. And they still don't have the foggiest idea what the church is.

Christian people are generally as confused as their pastors. Many of them know only that the "churches" of their acquaintance are a far cry from what God intended. That's why literally millions of people who profess to be Christians are more or less alienated from the organized church. We live in a society that is coming to tremendously encouraging conclusions about God and Jesus Christ. However, the conclusions of that same society about the church are not encouraging.[1]

That particular dichotomy bothers me. Why does our culture have one opinion of Jesus and an altogether different opinion of the church? The Bible teaches that the church is the Body of Christ (see Eph. 1:22-23) and that "in this world we are like him" (1 John 4:17). When people differentiate between the church and Christ, when they say, "We're going to write off the church, but we surely do love and believe in Jesus," something is seriously wrong.

I believe that we in the church need to face that situation and its implications. To the extent that we do so, the Holy Spirit can teach us how to restructure or conceive of the church so that there is no great gap between the way that we see the church in the world and the way we see Christ in the world. Toward this end, I want to put before you two models of the church. One model I call the "church as a field," the other is the "church as a force."

The Church as a Field

Do you think of the church as an organized, corporate structure located in the community at a specific address? Something to which you can direct people? Something identified and visible? Maybe with a steeple and maybe not, but a definitely located entity? That's a partial description of the church as a field.

In the church-as-a-field concept, the organized church is where the people come to do the work of God. A farmer's field is where he plants his crops and does his work. Just so, the field, as it relates to the church, is the arena in which the church does its work. Whatever is to be done by the church is done there.

This concept—that the field is where the work is done—is crucial. You see, Jesus said, "The field is the world" (Matt. 13:38). From that, it follows that the work of the church is to be done *in the world*. When we think that the believer's meeting place is where the work is to be done, we have departed from the concept Jesus originally established. Instead of the world being the field, we have made the church the field.

This concept of the church as a field will determine or at least temper all that the church does. Let's consider how the field mentality affects the church in its emphasis, goals, ministry and motivation, and then we'll consider some of the end results. The following description may be something of a caricature. It may exaggerate some features, and few churches probably fit the description completely. But I think the description will strike pretty close to home for many.

What Does the Church as a Field Emphasize?

When we see the church building as the place where the work of God is to be done, we develop the kinds of emphases that will get people into that building.

First, we need a great deal of visibility. The church must be prominently located. People must see it and preferably should have to pass it daily on their way to school, work and shopping. After all, how will they ever get there if they don't know where it is? Not only must the church be obvious, but the leaders of the church must also take on a significant public relations role. (I'm not against public relations, but sometimes this becomes a primary focus in this concept of the church.) Because the church has to be visible, the leadership—whether the pastor, the associate or whoever—must get into the community primarily to bring about this visibility.

Second, the happenings that take place inside this building must be of such a nature that people will be attracted to it. Program and promotion become very important. A high-powered program and strong promotion, of course, demand a great deal of effort, money and organization, so the church's emphases become visibility, organization, program and promotion. I'm not saying that these are bad; I'm just questioning their validity as priorities. Is this really what the church is all about?

These are the main emphases in this concept of the church. We give a great deal of attention to these things, because we see the building as the place where action is.

What Goals Does the Church as a Field Have?

The goals of the church as a field are defined in terms of numbers in attendance, budget and facility. Those things make up our concept of success in this model simply because success is the attainment of our goals. The primary purpose of the church as a field is to grow. Of course, the goals are flexible. If we are not reaching great numbers, then we change our success semantics from quantity to quality. We're after a few good men. And we've handled the success problem.

Budget? Obviously, it takes money to run a church. But when this becomes our goal, we have seriously confused means and ends. When we operate the church in order to get money enough to operate the church, we shouldn't be too surprised that people write off the church as something that is unlike Christ.

Facility is vitally important to the concept of the church as a field because the only way to increase the field is by enlarging the facility. If we are going to do a great work for God and it's all within the building, then we must have an enormous building.

How Does the Church as a Field Accomplish Its Ministry?

An interesting point here is that the church as a field does not have an adequate description of what its ministry is. Its ministry, so far, is to get people into the building, because that is where the work of God is done. Its primary ministry is to grow.

Once the people are gathered, this work centers around a professional. If people are going to be prayed for, then the professional is going to be the person who does it because he has the professional hands. And when there are more heads than his hands can take care of, we add another professional. So now we have four hands instead of two. As the field increases, we have more heads than four hands can handle, so we add another professional. And then we departmentalize the professionals so that we have hands in every area of the members' lives. What we are doing is setting up a rather stringent kind of professional approach to ministry.

A second interesting aspect about this kind of ministry is that the arrows all go in. By this, I mean that the organization is endeavoring to pull people out of the culture into the church. Everything we do is designed to draw people. We have contests, prizes and outreach campaigns. We give away iPods, videos, cell phones, a weekend at a golf resort . . . anything, just get them in. Because this is where the action is.

Ministry becomes a positional identity within the organization. That is, if people are going to minister, they must be director of something or minister of something or associate of something. They will have a title and a position within the organizational structure. As a result, individual members are easily misled about the meaning of Christian service and are often reduced to spectators. Once they're in the field, unless they win a position, they have little relevance except to help keep the machine going. They keep the seats occupied and invite their neighbors, but that's not fulfilling, so they become a bit confused. Then they either grab for power or drop out. Or they regress into a support or nonsupport role of the pastor's program. A lot of pastoral opposition stems from this kind of frustration in people's lives.

What Motivates the Church as a Field?

Basically, the motivation of the church as a field is to get people in. That is called "evangelism." And once we have them in we must keep them in, because if we don't, the field is going to shrink. So we design elaborate programs to keep the people there, which results in an enormous amount of programming. We had to program to get the people, and now we have to program to keep them.

It is also important to get people serving the church. The reason that this is absolutely necessary in this model is that the church is the field. Therefore, if people are to serve the Lord at all, they are going to be doing it within the organization. The other subtle but paralyzing fact is that as the organization continues to grow, it becomes cannibalistic. It eats up resources, energy and, ultimately, people. It ceases to be a means and becomes an end. It no longer serves the purpose of the ministry; it *is* the purpose of the ministry.

A subtle thing happens in our mentality if we are not careful. We begin to exploit people. We're reaching people not because they are hurting, but because they can help us in our church endeavors. *Just think—if that man with all his money would join, he could do a lot for this church.* Suddenly, the integrity of our motives is eroded, and that's a very dangerous thing. It means that at some point we are going to start hurting people. People are going to get chewed up in the machine.

In our church, we pick up pieces of people who have been chewed up in such religious machines—people who have been hurt, who hate religion, hate the preacher, hate everything to do with the church package. Many of them have a real case. It's not that anyone wants to hurt people. No pastor is in the ministry to hurt people. I've had pastors come and weep in my office, saying, "I like people. I want to help them. I've spent my life trying to help people, but it seems that at some point they get hurt." Often, these pastors have been under such pressure to make the machine hum that they have allowed the people to suffer.

When the church is the field, we are also motivated to compete with family, school, television and something called "the world." That is no small task, but we must do it. Why? Because we have to rip people away from other things and get them occupied with the church program.

What Are the Dangers of this Approach to Church Life?

First, the pastoral role is distorted and misdirected. In evangelical churches, the pastor tends to become the center of the operation. Some men have the charisma to carry that role well. Their platform manner magnetizes people. In personal relationships, they exude charm and self-confidence. As administrators, they rival the top executives in big business. But let's face it: there aren't many of those around.

Under some ecclesiastical systems, the pastor tends to become a puppet instead of a star. He doesn't have enough autonomy as a leader to take hold of things and make them happen. He has too many boards between him and what he wants to accomplish. So he becomes a political puppet, compromising everywhere and just trying to keep everybody happy. That's also frustrating. Whether a pastor becomes a star or a puppet, he is being misdirected. His true role is to be neither of those. Rather, he is to be an equipper of the saints.

Even more frightening than what happens to the pastor is what happens to the church. Again, the tendency is to go in one of two directions. The end result is usually either mediocrity or sub-culturization. Let's trace out how it works.

Notice that we're talking end results here. The church as a field may show absolutely no marks of mediocrity at the beginning. To the contrary, there may be great first-generation excitement. That group of people on whom the church was founded is blessed of God. They are excited, things are moving, the budget's always met, the building is coming along, and new people are present every Sunday. Everyone is awake. Hallelujah!

But the second generation is different. I'm not referring to the children of the first generation—I'm talking about the second wave of people who make up a church after it is well established. The building is complete. The income is adequate. The organization is functioning. The church settles into what I call a "second-generation compromise." Everyone is quite comfortable now. The church program is going along nicely. The time for personal sacrifice is past. The people get to sit back and enjoy the fruits of their labors—or the labors of the first generation.

The stage is set for third-generation mediocrity. Nothing much is happening anymore. Faces change as people and pastors come and go, but that's about it. Even desperate attempts to shake things up, to get moving again, have little effect. Pastors get discouraged and leave or settle into mediocrity along with the church. They sort of retire early, so to speak, and give up hope of anything significant happening, but they stick with the routine anyhow. It's a living.

God help the poor pastor who ends up with third-generation mediocrity. But frankly, I think that's where most pastors are. That's why they shuffle. They trade this pastorate and its mediocrity for that pastorate and its mediocrity. They get about a year-and-a-half honeymoon out of it and then start looking for another church. Mediocrity is always looking for a way out. Give some release and it may honeymoon with you for a while, but it always has a way of settling back down if you don't change basic concepts. The only hope is the rise of a new superstar who can capture the day and move the church on to bigger and better things and lead the people over the top for Jesus.

If the church as a field does not end with mediocrity, it will end in subculturization. Or it may be both mediocre and subculturized. A subculture is a separate system within a system. It defines its own lifestyle, has its own speech, and tends to externalize its basic spiritual qualities. It develops its own community. When a church subculturizes, it becomes, as one writer put it, "an island of irrelevance in a sea of despair."

That is, I think, a great danger for the Christian church. I see great segments of the church going in that direction or already there. The tendency always is to establish a community in which there is uniformity. That way, we don't have to worry about error or non-predictability creeping in. So the church tends, on the wave of revival, to take the result of that revival and institutionalize it. Years later the institution remains, but the life has long gone.

We tried to go the subculture route at East Hill in the early days. We didn't know any better. We had a close-knit group of about 10 families, and our basic aim was to solve all our own problems, keep our group intact and add to our little community. But someone would always come in who didn't look as we did, didn't talk as we talked, and didn't give a hang about our little community. We were always needing to convert these people to our community concept.

Finally, we began to get the message. I was praying one day for the Lord to give me the community, and the Lord stopped me. "Never pray for that again," He said. "I am not going to give a community to you. Instead, I want you to pray, 'Lord, give me to the community.'" This was how I finally awoke to the fact that God didn't want us to be a separate subculture, He wanted us to penetrate every segment of the society in which He had placed us.

Jesus said, "You are the salt of the earth" (Matt. 5:13). Salt, to have any effect at all, must be mixed in with the substance that needs salt. Nobody but a collector sets up saltshakers and admires them. A subcultured church is like a saltshaker on display.

Whether the church as a field leads to mediocrity on the one hand or to a Christian subculture on the other, the result is the same. The world concludes that religion may be okay for some but that it's irrelevant to real life. And Christianity is just another irrelevant religion.

Obviously, these are gross generalizations. But these are concepts one must work through to arrive at any adequate definition of the church.

The Church as a Force

The church is people, redeemed, filled with the Holy Spirit, equipped to serve, meeting needs everywhere in Jesus' name. Do not underestimate the preceding statement. That concept of the church will affect everything: the way the pastor preaches, the way the church is organized and promoted, the way the program develops, and the way the building is designed. This concept of the church is so decisive that if you don't see it in the thoroughgoing context I have just suggested, you will not understand what I am saying.

Among other things, I'm saying that we need to direct the church away from professionalism and into the hands of people who do not know what they are doing. I can say from firsthand experience that this policy is both scary and at times utterly ridiculous, but always, in my mind, necessary.

As we did with the church as a field, let's examine the emphases, goals, ministry and motivation of the church as a force and consider the results.

What Does the Church as a Force Emphasize?

In this concept of the church, the field is the world, as Jesus said. That is where the work is to be done. The emphases in the church-as-a-field model are visibility, organization, program and promotion. The church as a force emphases are worship, training and fellowship, because *these are the things that produce Spirit-filled people who can meet others' needs in Jesus' name.*

When our people gather on Sundays or at other times, they are not the church at work. To attend services is not to serve the Lord. The primary work of the church is not to meet, though we are told not to forsake doing so. The church meeting is not the church working; it is simply the church meeting. Services are for what we might call R and R, rest and restoration, and this includes worship and celebration. We get together, we sing, we clap, we praise God, we worship, we meet one another and talk about Jesus. We don't hear any profanity or dirty stories. It's tremendous. It's unadulterated fun and enjoyment in a pure, clean and loving environment.

When we meet, we read the Bible, and the Lord speaks to us in various ways. Brothers and sisters more gifted than in certain areas minister to us. We thoroughly enjoy it. We're healed. Our lives are changed. We receive great spiritual blessings. Why? So that we can gather for a repeat performance on Thursday night because by then we'll need to be pumped up again? No! The church is rested and restored at meetings so that they can work in the world when they leave.

The church is at work right now. People are sitting in board meetings where they are employed. They are driving taxis and trucks and buses. They are meeting in council chambers, in the legislature, in commissioners' offices. They are teaching classes. They are milking cows. They are changing diapers. They are all over the community. So when we get together the next time, we'll share what's been going on. We'll rejoice together over our victories and pray about our needs. Some are going to be present who were touched by that work of the church out in the world. They are going to begin to understand what Jesus' lifestyle is all about. It's a powerful thing.

We worship, we pray, we fellowship, we learn.

What Goals Does the Church as a Force Set?

The church as a field has goals expressed in numbers, budget and facility. The church as a force has goals that are personal and individual: we want each member to come to *wholeness*, be *equipped* and be *released* into the world to minister. Our basic assumption is that the Holy Spirit who fills the pastor can fill every believer to whom the pastor preaches. And each believer is potentially capable of ministering just as surely as the pastor is, though perhaps in a different way.

The role of a pastor is to help Christians start living in the light of the truth. Christians tend to have a lot of theology in their hearts and a good bit in their heads, but not much in their feet. Christianity that doesn't walk around in shoes isn't worth much. It has to walk in shoes, in all kinds of shoes—sandals, boots, high heels and flip-flops. It has to walk. The role of a pastor is to teach people how to get their Christianity to walk right. If we only teach people how to think Christianly and feel it but not how to walk it, then we are failing.

Most church members are content to watch the pastor walk. "Pastor made 435 calls this month!" And the poor pastor. He is chewing Rolaids. He's on Prilosec. His cheeks are sunken. His face has a yellow pallor. And the people come on Sunday mornings and get upset because he doesn't feed them steak. The best he can do is serve a little warmed-over soup. He's been busy doing their work. Do you follow me? It's not the job of the pastor to minister to every need in the church. The job of the pastor is to teach everybody in the church how to minister.

The Bible says that pastors are supposed to "prepare God's people for works of service, so that the body of Christ may be built up" (Eph. 4:12). Take careful notice of this Scripture, for it is foundational to the concept of the church as a force. Preparing God's people—that's the pastors' job, and that's a whole different ball game from them doing the ministry themselves. The church needs to place its members in a healing environment of love, acceptance and forgiveness. It must bring people to wholeness in such an environment, equip them, and then release them.

What is the Ministry of the Church as a Force?

The automatic result of great healing is great outreach. As people come to wholeness, they minister. Other people are touched.

When the church is a force, the ministry-by-professionals-only tendency of the church as a field yields to a ministry by all the believers. Along with this comes an altering, even a dissolution, of the traditional lay-clergy role. That is easy to say, but it's hard to do in an established church. People don't know how to let it happen. They don't know how to cope with a pastor who actually expects the people to carry on the ministry. They almost demand that the pastor do the work.

The breakdown of the clergy-layman distinction is also frightening for pastors. They are losing their safety zone and feel vulnerable. People know that they are as human as anyone else, though they happen to be pastors. That's very threatening to some. They fear they will not be respected any longer and that their leadership capability will be impaired. Many are even taught in seminary not to be friends with church members—to keep a "healthy distance" from the people.

Pastors are, in fact, as human and fallible as anyone else. Why play charades then? What good is leadership that must depend on falsehood for its strength?

I do not believe in vertical relationships in the church. I do not believe in the emergence of an elite in the church. I do not believe that I have power over anyone simply by virtue of the fact that I am a pastor. The only way I can function as pastor in anyone's life is if that person lets me. If he or she doesn't want me to, there is not a thing I can do. I have no power to make anyone bend. I could threaten people. I could set up a system of political pressure. But as a pastor, I must make it one-on-one with people. In order to do that, I must be an authentic person. That means I must take the risk of being open and transparent.

Being open is scary, and in some fellowships it is downright risky, as James D. Mallory, Jr. describes:

One time in a Sunday school class on love within the family, Betsy (my wife) admitted she sometimes had hateful feelings toward me or the children. The other members of the class clearly were not used to such honesty and immediately hid behind a pious cloak, suggesting they should pray for poor Betsy, who obviously was in dire straits as a Christian.

Many are afraid to take the type of risk Betsy took because others might think they are not very good Christians if they admit some of the foolish things they do and the destructive thoughts and feelings they have.

Betsy's honesty in the class ultimately paid off, however, and others began to share some of their problems. They began to function as the body of Christ should function. They could pray honestly and specifically for each other.[2]

In the church as a force, there is a climate of love, acceptance and forgiveness. The pastor is not living a life of pretense as if he or she were somehow different and better than others. These two elements alone do much to make the church a healing fellowship in which our Betsys and everyone else can be real and open.

In the church as a force, the pastoral leadership is also constantly endeavoring to facilitate the ministry of the congregation. This means that the pastor carefully avoids usurping that ministry. He or she does not do the work for the people but involves them in doing it themselves.

A man once asked me to pray with him about his living situation. He lived in a large apartment complex and felt like Lot in Sodom because of the things going on there. He really wanted to move. Our church could have responded to this situation in a number of different ways. For one, we could have built and operated our own apartments. Financially, we could have handled that with no problem. We had already been approached with that proposal and had property on which to build. But that was not our choice.

However, I couldn't just say to that man, "No, I'm not going to pray with you. Sit there and tough it out." So I said, "Listen, you are not there by accident. Let's begin to work and facilitate some ministry for you. Let's pray. Let's fast, and we'll see what the Lord says to us."

I soon discovered that a lot of other people in our church were in similar circumstances. One Sunday night after service, we gathered everyone who lived in apartments, a whole roomful of people. I said, "How many of you feel like you want to move?" Many raised their hands. I said, "Why don't we stop asking God for a place to move and start asking Him for a way to infect the place we live? How can we have such a case of Christianity that we become an epidemic?"

They just lit up. The first thing they wanted was for me to appoint a staff member to come and teach a Bible study at their places. I said, "No, I'm not about to do that. That's crazy. Why increase the staff? You live there. How many of you are filled with the Holy Spirit?"

Then they thought I was saying, "Go down by the pool every Sunday morning, set up a pulpit, open the Bible, and say 'thus saith the Lord!'" I was not saying that at all. "I'm simply saying to be open for business," I explained. "Now what does that mean to you?"

One fellow decided he could write out his testimony and post it on the bulletin board. He happened to be in charge of an apartment building for 400 adult students of Mt. Hood

Community College. He had been a bartender a few months before. So he posted his testimony on the bulletin board, where all the messages were. He attached a note that read, "If you want to talk about this, see me, manager's apartment." A steady stream of people began coming to him.

Now, wouldn't it have been foolish to put that man on staff? Or hire someone else as minister of apartment evangelism? Ministry is people filled with the Holy Spirit meeting the needs of other people in Jesus' name.

What is the Motivation of the Church as a Force?

What are we trying to accomplish in this model? We are trying to bring healing to the whole man, to every area of a person's life. We are not out to use or exploit people, as is the temptation in the church as a field. We become a healing agency in the community, not a place of refuge from the community. Nor do we compete with the world. We don't want to compete but to change values so that family, school, vocation, entertainment and the rest take their proper place.

For example, one exciting thing we developed at our church was the concept of parents and children spending 12 years or more together as a healing unit in the public school system. That, to me, was a fantastic alternative to starting our own schools. I'm not opposed to Christian schools, but I didn't think that was God's call to our particular church. I'm not against Christian colleges, but I think the believers who have had no Christian background should be the ones attending them. Christian people who have been in church all their lives ought to be the ones attending secular colleges.

As I was doing this 30-year update, I was asked the question, "How did this work out?" Actually, the results were

mixed. In some of our schools there was a tremendous openness to the parents who wanted to involve themselves. There
was an openness to the kids and their Christian views and
values. In those schools, we were able to have significant effect. But other schools were not open. Some were violently
opposed to anything that smacked of Christianity and re-
sisted any Christian influence.

In some cases, we counseled the parents to place their
children in a healthier environment. We were fortunate to
have Christian schools in our area that provided a good alternative. I do not believe in sacrificing our children on the
altar of a closed, anti-Christian or dangerous environment.
So you make the call. Where there is opportunity for influence, take it. But remember what Jesus told the disciples
when He sent them out to minister: if you find a closed door
and are not received, then leave (see Matt. 10:14). I think in
many cases we leave too soon—we encounter some opposition, some questions, some suspicion and cynicism and we
bolt—but, on the other hand, we have to be sure not to leave
too late for our kids. One thing we did do at our church was
to become aware of the Christian teachers and administrators in our schools and districts and find ways to encourage
and support them.

We are not in the world to compete but to change values.
I don't care whether every family in our church has a TV, a
computer, a cell phone or several. I do care that they understand their priorities enough to know what to do with these
things and that they teach and monitor their children to be
sure they do as well. That doesn't come from me going
through the TV guide with them each Sunday morning to
give them the recommended programs or place the approved dot-coms in the church bulletin.

What Are the Dangers of this Approach to Church Life?

The church-as-a-force concept is not without potential dangers. Most pastors get nervous when the ministry is placed in the hands of nonprofessionals. Ordinary people start going off in all directions, witnessing, caring and praying for the sick and distressed. The pastor may not even know about everything that's going on, and he or she may begin to feel that things are out of control. In fact, things are out of control, but a pastor does not need to be intimidated by this. In my own situation, I've decided that if only what I can control is allowed to happen through our congregation, not much will happen.

In the church as a force, the pastoral role is dynamic and in constant refinement. That is also threatening to some pastors. As the church is developing, the pastor's role is also developing within that context. In my church, I'm doing different things now than I did a year ago, and I never do arrive. I must keep on responding to what God is doing in the Body.

Another danger in the church as a force is the confusion that arises because of nontraditional structures and patterns of action. People who come to our church with the field mentality deeply ingrained do not understand us. We are always having to educate a new wave of people. In three years, we went from under 500 to about 3,000 in attendance. That gave us a big job to do in communicating the principles upon which our church was built.

Despite these and other possible dangers, the end results of the church as a force are wonderful. The true pastoral function—to equip the saints for the work of the ministry—is preserved. That is vitally important, for according to Scripture that is the only true function a pastor has. That's it. And as much as a pastor can dedicate himself or herself to that single work, that pastor is fulfilling his or her ministry.

Individual member ministry is also preserved under this model of the church, and that is also crucial. I've found that people get excited when they have a reason for being Christians other than keeping themselves out of hell. People get bored just waiting for heaven. So what do they do? They start complaining, griping and gossiping. The reason they are bored is that they don't know what they are saved for. They know what they are saved *from* and what they are saved *to,* but not what they are saved *for.*

Frankly, Christians get tired of hearing evangelistic sermons continually. Many pastors try to evangelize audiences made up of 99 percent Christians. "What if one sinner is there?" they ask. I reply that if one sinner is there and he can survive authentic praise and worship and fellowship, he is an amazing creature. If he can survive that, no sermon the pastor can preach will get to him.

Too often we are caught preaching to a minority while the majority are sitting there bored to death and wondering, *What in the world am I doing here?* The only thing that can justify their coming is to bring a sinner with them. Then they can go home and say, "Well, I sure didn't get anything out of that message, but at least the pastor talked to my neighbor."

The greatest criticism people make of their pastor is not that he or she doesn't love them or care for them but that he or she is not feeding them. That is terrifying when, in fact, the total role of the pastor is to equip the saints to do the work of the ministry. I always ask a few questions to see if they are really hungry from ministering or if they have become connoisseurs, checking each morsel to see if its flavored just right. It is a tough job to feed people who aren't hungry. People who don't minister do not work up a spiritual appetite.

When the saints start doing the ministry, they get excited, and the church truly becomes a force for God in the world.

Notes

1. Dan Kimball explores this idea in some depth in *They Like Jesus but Not the Church* (Grand Rapids, MI: Zondervan, 2007).

2. James D. Mallory, Jr. and Stanley Baldwin, *The Kink and I* (Wheaton, IL: Victor Books, 1973). Used by permission.

PEOPLE EQUIPPED TO SERVE

A young woman named Jackie, a fairly new Christian, walked into a major discount store in Portland. As she passed through the prescription area, she noticed a woman leaning on the counter, obviously very sick. Jackie felt an impulse to stop and pray with the woman, but she did what 90 percent of us would do and said to herself, *No, she would think I'm nuts.*

Jackie did her shopping and on the way out passed the prescription counter again. The woman was now seated in a chair, still obviously very ill. Again Jackie was impressed, *Go, talk to her, pray with her.*

Jackie started on out the door, but she just couldn't go. So she resigned herself to become the classic fool for Jesus. She went over, sat down beside the sick woman, took her by the hand and said, "I can see that you're quite sick, and I don't want you to think I'm imposing, but I'm a Christian. Would you mind if I prayed for you?"

The woman began to weep. She said, "I've been sick for so long."

Jackie just held her hand and with eyes open said, "Lord Jesus, I know You love this lady, and I know You don't want her to be sick. Just because You love her, heal her and show her how much You care."

That was it. They exchanged phone numbers and Jackie went home.

The next day, Jackie got a phone call from this woman asking her to come to the woman's house. Jackie went. The woman's husband had stayed home from work in order to meet Jackie. The prescription the woman got the day before was unopened on the kitchen table. The woman and her husband were both standing there weeping.

The woman said, "When I came home, I went to bed and slept all night. You know, I haven't slept all night for years." With her particular sickness, she slept only for short periods and had to get up to take medication. Her husband thought she had died. He came in and awakened her to ask if she was okay. She said that she felt great.

He said, "Well, you haven't taken your medicine."

She said, "I know, but I slept all night."

She then told her husband what had happened at the shopping center. So he wanted to meet Jackie.

The people knew practically nothing about the gospel. Jackie explained to them the love of Jesus, how they could be free from their sin, and how Jesus wants people well not only physically but on the inside. They both trusted in Jesus Christ.

Equipped in the Spirit

I believe Jackie's experience was an example of the gift of healing operating in the marketplace (literally, since it was at a shopping center). The gifts of the Spirit, as I understand them, are God's means of getting to people and meeting their needs through believers. I do not believe that spiritual gifts were meant primarily for the sanctuary. Some of them can operate there, and that's fine, but many of them were primarily designed for the street.

The Bible says that there are many different kinds of gifts but one Spirit (see 1 Cor. 12:4). The word *gift* here is *charisma*, which means an extension of grace. How is the grace of God extended in this world? Through these charismas, these gifts, these abilities. That's how we extend the grace of God. Do you realize that when you speak the wisdom of God to someone you are exercising a spiritual gift, even though you might not realize it?

We sometimes seem to think that a trumpet should blow and a quivering voice should break forth, "Thus saith the Lord. Okay, we're going to have a prophecy now." Can you imagine going out in public and doing that? Do you see anyone in the New Testament functioning that way in the exercise of the gift of prophecy? Not one. It's not there. Why bottle the gift of prophecy in a wineskin that won't work outside the sanctuary—and have it so frightening in the sanctuary that people not initiated into the club see it and run out scared half to death? Even in theologies that allow for the gifts of the Spirit today, there has been a reaction against the extreme and emotionalized staging of them. Consequently, they are downplayed or ignored.

I believe in the gifts of the Spirit. If there ever was a time we needed the supernatural presence of Jesus in our world, it is now. But I do not believe in some holy-sounding voice, religious language, hype or grand performance that calls attention to our great giftedness. Jesus ministered supernaturally in very natural ways—ways that fit wherever He happened to be: the road, a meeting, the synagogue, a cemetery, a market, a wedding, a dinner, anywhere and every-where He was.

I believe that in our conversations with people who are questioning and confused, we can prophesy or give a word of wisdom to that person and not even know the Spirit has used us. Later, we think, *Wow, where did I get that insight? Where's my notebook? I should write that down.*

My wife, Barbara, and I were on a road trip to a beautiful part of our state. We had just parked at a lake lodge to get lunch when someone called my name. Bob and Carol were from our church, and they had seen us pull in and came over to say hi. As Bob and I were talking, Carol was telling Barb of her frustration about not being able to sell their home. They wanted to move to Portland but couldn't until they sold their house. It had been on the market a long time, and she was getting a little disgusted with God that He wasn't showing more interest in their problem. She was discouraged and wondering if she had done something to displease Him.

When our conversations flowed back together, she referred briefly to this issue she was having with God. I responded with an off-hand comment that, frankly, I had never made before and was quite surprised when it just kind of came out. "I'm not sure God cares that much about where you live. He is with you and loves you wherever you are." It was a little shocking to hear myself say this, because both Barb and I are sure He directed us to the house we are now living in. The comment just sort of passed on into the rest of the conversation. We said our goodbyes, and they drove on their way.

About two hours later, they came back into the parking lot as we were getting ready to leave. Carol jumped out of their car and came rushing up to me, crying. "You said something that really upset me," she said. "But when I thought and prayed about it, I realized you were right. God doesn't care about *where* Bob and I live right now. He cares about *how* we live. That had never occurred to me. I understand now and am completely at peace. It is enough that He is with us."

Her anger toward God was gone. Her worry about selling the house was gone . . . and all because the Holy Spirit decided to slip a little prophetic comment into a casual conversation, set her free from anxiety, and affirm His love for her.

Christian people by and large don't know what gifts they have because they don't see them in action in the everyday world. They hear about gifts and perhaps see a display at a meeting, but they don't see the pastor or anyone else ministering in the marketplace. They see gifts being exercised only by professionals and in sanctuary settings. That concept has to be broken down. There is nothing that Jesus did when He walked on this earth that He cannot do through any Christian. But people don't know it, don't know what to do about it, and aren't trusted by the leadership to go ahead and get it done.

What I'm saying is this: *people who are filled with the Holy Spirit are already basically equipped for ministry.* What the church needs to do is help people to understand this truth, not mislead them into thinking they are somehow unqualified to serve.

Christianity is not difficult to communicate. It's simple. We make it hard by our extreme efforts. We give soul-winning courses that take eight weeks or eight months to complete. This communicates to our people how difficult it is to win anyone to Christ. As a result, Christians are scared to death to tell anybody about Jesus. They memorize every possible question any non-Christian could ask as well as the correct answers, just to make sure they have all the bases covered. When they have done that, we tell them they are equipped. They aren't equipped; they are incapacitated. We have them so intent on nailing people with the Bible and giving answers to them that they forget there is a person there—hurting.

Maybe the correct answer does not help. Maybe what a friend or neighbor needs is a cup of coffee and an arm around his or her shoulder. Someone to listen and care. Someone to exercise the greatest spiritual gift of all: love. It doesn't take a professional to love.

We call in experts from all over the country to teach about the Holy Spirit. This communicates to our people how difficult it is to be filled with the Spirit. We hire evangelists from all over the world to come and conduct healing campaigns. This communicates that only an expert can minister healing. We have seminars and conferences on every conceivable subject. They can be helpful, I suppose, but too often we are communicating that living supernaturally in a natural way is technical and difficult. Any believer filled with the Spirit has the supernatural power of Jesus to meet any situation and put any demonic power to flight. The name of Jesus is powerful in the mouth of a believer. It's not more powerful in one person's mouth than it is in the mouth of any other believer.

We make specialties out of ministry. We make Christian service difficult. Ministry is the natural flow of Jesus' life through us, even when we may not be aware of it.

Rob, a friend of mine, went into a local car dealership to buy a car. Now, that has to be the one experience that is the least spiritual and the most frustrating. Rob knew the car he wanted and what he could afford to pay. Then the salesperson came over, and you know the drill. . . . Rob, however, remained calm. He treated the salespeople with kindness and consideration. He laughed and joked with them. He even had more serious conversations about some personal things.

As you know, whenever you go to buy a car, several people get involved in the process. Rob did the same with the salesman, the manager and the financial person, right down the line. They were all thoroughly enjoying each other, and the usual tension of negotiating was completely absent. The whole thing took about an hour. When the deal was finished, a man came out of one of the windowed offices and asked Rob to come in for a minute. He turned out to be the owner of the dealership and, unknown to Rob, had been watching the entire process.

"I know who you are," he began. (Rob was on the staff of a local church.) "I am not a Christian and have not been in church for many years. But as I sat watching the way you treated my staff and the joy you brought to the entire store . . . your consideration and kindness . . . it was like I was watching Jesus out there, and I had to talk with you."

The owner then proceeded to pour out the anguish in his life right then and asked Rob if he would pray for him. That day, the owner began a relationship with Jesus and with my friend Rob that continues to this day.

Now, it seems to me that if you can be Jesus when you are buying a car, you are the real deal.

The leadership of the church has sinned against the Body of Christ by communicating to God's people that they are not fit to serve Him. I still remember the day when I had to get out of my chair in my office and fall flat on my face on the rug, asking God to forgive me, because He had showed me clearly that I would be held responsible for every ministry I stole from my people. And I had a list of them. I asked God to show me how to avoid that in the future.

I still fail sometimes. The pressure of wanting things to work is great. We have to be bigger this year than we were last year. But in the name of getting the job done, we must not take the ministry away from the people whom God intends to do it.

Confining the operation of spiritual gifts to the sanctuary or to professionals is consistent with the church-as-a-field mentality. But it is not consistent with the church as a force. More important, it is not consistent with Scripture.

Equipped in the Word

We have said that people who are filled with the Holy Spirit are basically equipped for ministry. What they need beyond that is to be equipped in the Word. By that I don't mean they must learn the proof texts they can use to club sinners into submission. I mean they must learn the biblical principles that will make them what they ought to be as Christians.

Truth must be communicated to people, and that is accomplished primarily through simple, direct teaching of God's Word. The place to begin is to teach people who they are in Jesus—positional truth. *Who am I?* They are more than simply a sinner saved. *What does saved mean? What are the implications of that?* (Ephesians is great on this.) Once people begin to understand who they are and what they have, they will try the concepts out. When this process gets under way, the pastor will have to run to keep up with the people instead of always trying to cook up some way to get them moving.

I am convinced that pure, raw, direct exposure to the Word of God will absolutely change people's lives. In fact, many pastors would do their congregations a favor if they would stop trying to preach and just sit down, open the Bible, and read it aloud. You can bet that 90 percent of the people aren't reading it for themselves.

We did a phenomenal thing in our services: we read the book of Revelation. I was so tired of charts. I was as confused as everyone else from all the theories trying to explain this book.

They only made it more indecipherable than ever. Yet Revelation 1:3 says, "Blessed is the one who reads the words of this prophecy, and blessed are those who hear it and take to heart what is written in it." I noticed that it does not say, "Blessed is he who understands it all or figures it out a little better than the next guy."

I had found that the first book the typical newborn child of God wants to read is Revelation. I often thought, *The dirty devil wants to get them confused.* But one day another thought barged in: *Don't you think that desire may be born of the Holy Spirit?*

"Lord, why on earth would You take a newborn baby to the book of Revelation—with its beasts and demons and weird stuff?" I protested.

In the midst of that little exchange, the Lord said, "I want you to read the book of Revelation to your congregation, and don't you dare do an exposition on it." The only thing I was allowed to do besides read was to define terminology so that everyone understood what the Scripture was saying. That's all. No expository explanation of any kind, no charts, no books, no dates, no numerology, no cross-references and no theorizing.

We spent six weeks as a congregation reading the book of Revelation every Sunday evening. The place was packed. I almost felt guilty for not preaching. We would read and read, laugh and weep, and wonder. We did not learn who the Antichrist is. We did not date the Rapture. We did not get into the tribulation and millennium controversies. I have a position on all those issues, but who cares? I rather think we are all going to be saying on the way up, "Wait a minute—this isn't supposed to happen now. My chart says so and so." The Lord will just wink at Gabriel and say, "See there, I told them they wouldn't know the time, but they didn't believe me."

I don't think any of our prophecy experts have it figured out right. If one of them did happen to stumble onto the exact plan, I wouldn't be surprised if the Lord changed things a little, just so that guy wouldn't have all eternity to brag about it.

We simply read Revelation. When we got through, we had a phenomenal concept of the *power of Jesus,* of the *sovereignty of God,* of the *security that is ours* on this planet, and of the utter, complete, unquestionable *triumph of the church* of Jesus Christ. On that last night, the congregation stood together with uplifted hands and praised the Lord for nearly half an hour. It was one of the most powerful things I have ever seen. *That's why the Lord takes new Christians to the book of Revelation. What does a new Christian need to know more than those four things?*

We read through the book of Acts the same way. Then we read the book of James.

My primary emphasis in teaching is to life-relate the Word. To do that, I must be immersed in the Word. I must live it. Its principles have to be mine. To this end, at a minimum I read the book of Psalms, the book of Proverbs and the entire New Testament every 30 days. That sounds like a lot of reading, but it is actually only 10 to 14 pages a day, depending on your Bible. It takes an average of a half hour a day, the equivalent of one TV newscast or situation comedy. It is so simple to cover an enormous amount of Scripture that way. Do it every 30 days, and what happens? The Word gets worked into your system. You are immersed in biblical content. Then you add to your reading whatever you want from the Old Testament and other books.

Added to my daily systematic exposure to the Word are my times of extended study. Once every two months, or at least every three months, I take two to four days totally away from my situation. I grab some orange juice and take off for the hills where my cell phone won't work and nothing can bother me. I can't stand to eat my cooking, so I don't worry about food. It's not a big fasting thing for me. I like orange juice, so I take a couple of bottles of that—and immerse myself in the Word.

All I take to read is a Bible and a linguistic help—a Greek testament and lexicon, perhaps. I take no commentaries. I don't want my thinking restricted or my preaching to be just a revamp of someone else's ideas. A lot of pastors would save time and energy for everyone concerned if they just told their congregation what website they were downloading from and let them do it themselves.

At the other extreme from pastors who parrot one another are those who knock themselves out trying to be creative and original. These pastors sometimes fall into sensationalism or strange far-out interpretations of Scripture. The quickest and most valid way to originality is to just be yourself. You see, I am an original, and so are you. As I "forgive" myself for being as I am—as I learn to trust God's good judgment in creating me as He did and begin to accept myself—I am original. I can't help it. God has put my brain together and tutored it so that no one else can pick up the Word and see exactly what I see in it.

For me, good preaching is opening the Word and communicating to the people what I see. That's all it is. I do not need to be quotable. I'm not even interested in being quotable. I want my preaching to be walkable. "All Scripture is God-breathed and is useful for teaching, rebuking, correcting and training in righteousness, so that the man of God may be thoroughly equipped for every good work" (2 Tim. 3:16-17). That's what I'm about—equipping the saints to work. And there is no way to do that but through teaching the Word.

RELEASED TO MINISTER

When our church was very small, I sat around in my office reading and looking busy and hoping something would happen. Some of the concepts of the church as a force had begun to penetrate my mind. I realized the New Testament teaches that believers are to be the ministers, but I didn't understand how I could get from where I was to where I should be in that regard.

A phone call came one day from a woman who had been a Christian for only two or three weeks. She said, "I've been talking to my neighbor, and she wants to receive Christ. Could you come and talk to her?"

I said, "sure," walked out, got in my car and started down the road. I had gone no more than five or six blocks when the Lord began to interrupt me. I knew in a flash what He was saying: "If you go there, I will honor my word and on the basis of her trust in me that woman will be saved, but I will hold you responsible for stealing the reward of one of my sheep."

I said, "I don't understand. She is going to get saved, and I am going to be judged?"

It didn't make sense. Nevertheless, the Lord's word to me was so strong and so definite that I knew I couldn't go. I turned around and went back to my office.

On the way back, I got a short but intensive course in pastor-people relations. I remembered a deep-sea fishing trip my wife, Barbara, and I had taken. She had tied into a shark out there—a big one about eight feet long. She was having a ball trying to play out the shark. About that time, one of the crew members came, took her rod and landed the shark for her. What a letdown. He had taken away her victory, and she resented it.

The Lord said, "Jerry, that's exactly what you've been doing as a pastor. You have been running in, taking away the ministry of the people, thinking you're doing them a favor. But I'm going to judge you for stealing their ministry."

Having Faith in the Gospel

I called the woman on the phone, told her I couldn't come and explained why.

"But I don't know what to do," she said. "I don't know what to say."

"Do you know Jesus?" I said.

"Well, yes."

"If you know someone, you can introduce that person to anyone, can't you? What happened when you were introduced to Jesus? Were any Scriptures used? You could use those same verses if you want to. Just introduce your neighbor to Jesus the same way you were introduced to Him. If it worked for you, it will work for her."

She agreed to try it, and we had prayer together on the phone. Less than an hour later, there came a knock on my study door. Here stood this woman and her neighbor, both glowing as if they had spotlights on their faces. Not only had the neighbor been gloriously saved, but both women had also begun to understand that leading people to Christ is not the exclusive work of a few well-trained professionals. Any Christian can do it.

In fact, the gospel is so simple that even a non-Christian can lead another person to Christ. I've known it to happen. A man who was a member of our church for a number of years was a former drug pusher. He was led to Christ in a drug house in downtown Portland. One day, a girl from Spokane and this guy were smoking dope together. He said to her, "I'd like to be free of this dope."

The girl was not a Christian, but she had been raised in a Christian home. She said to him, "I know how you can do that. If you were to trust in Jesus as your Savior, He would deliver you."

"What?" he said. "What does all that mean?"

"I'm not going to tell you," she said.

"Why not?"

"Because then you'll take off and be a Christian, and I won't see you anymore."

He kept prodding her until finally she said, "All right, I'll tell you." She quoted John 3:16 and explained how to be saved. The man went into the other room and prayed to receive Christ. He walked out of that place and never went back. She stayed, and as far as I know is not a Christian to this day. This girl wasn't saved, didn't want to be saved, and didn't want him to be saved. Yet she was able to tell the way of salvation, and the power of the gospel transformed a man.

The power is in the gospel, not in the presentation or the delivery. Paul said, "I am not ashamed of the gospel, because it is the power of God for the salvation of everyone who believes" (Rom. 1:16). Do you see what our problem is? We who represent the gospel don't have enough faith in its power to believe what Paul said about it. Incredible!

Trusting the Life of Christ in People

Besides lacking faith in the gospel, there is among us a tragic distrust of the life of Christ in other believers. We are scared to death that they are going to goof things up, whether through incompetence or moral or spiritual failure. So we don't release them to minister. When it comes to incompetence, it is true that believers do sometimes goof. This sort of failure is not limited to the untrained, however, as we so-called professionals well know. But fail or not, we must delegate ministry to people, because that is God's plan.

If we give away ministry to someone and they make a mistake, we can clean it up together. That's all right. We all make a few mistakes along the way. The only people who don't make mistakes are those who never do anything. We've had enough of those people in the church in the past. They don't make the church a force.

God is big enough to turn even our goofs into something positive. I believe the Holy Spirit sees to it that the mistakes believers make in sincerely seeking to serve Him are not fatal to His kingdom or fatal to other people. We can trust Him.

Some pastors won't let the people minister because they feel it compromises the excellence of the church's program. Nobody else does the job well enough, so the pastor or some other trained professional must do it himself. The fact is that nobody really wants to do sloppy work. We need to help people to do their tasks well. But to say that they are not trainable—that no one can do it well enough but us—seems clearly to be an ego problem.

One pastor was such an organized perfectionist that his daughter remarked, "Even his parties have to have four points and a conclusion." It all comes back to our basic purpose. Are we out to produce flawless graphics and professional-looking performances? Or are we committed to producing people who can minister for Christ and who are actually involved in doing it?

If we are building people, we have to let them learn by doing. We can't be jumping in all the time and taking the rod from their hands lest they lose the fish or, worse, not letting them fish in the first place. We can't insulate people from possible embarrassment and defeat, for to do so sends the message that we don't trust them and that we think they are incompetent. That message translates directly into their belief about their ability to minister effectively outside the church walls.

The measure of our success as a church is not necessarily how many people we have but what is happening to those who are there, whether few or many. Every pastor needs to ask himself, *Where do I want the people in my congregation to be in their personal development one year from now, or five years from now?* Then they can work toward something far more meaningful than having a well-oiled machine. The pastor can work toward what God has called him or her to do: perfect the saints.

Besides a basic mistrust of people's competence, I also see among many Christians a tragic mistrust of the life of Christ in His people so far as their moral and spiritual commitment is concerned. Some seem to think they must put all kinds of hedges around Christians to keep them on the "straight and narrow." I don't understand this idea. The people in my congregation *don't want to sin.* They love Jesus, and they are trying to follow Him, just as I love Him and try to follow Him. These people don't need a warden to guard them; they need a shepherd to guide them. And when they do sin, they need love, acceptance and forgiveness, not suspicion and rejection. Pastors should be building the confidence of the people in the life of Christ within them, not tearing it down.

One man in our congregation who had not been a Christian for long came to me and asked me to pray that he would find a different job. "The place I work is so rotten you wouldn't believe it," he said. "I hear nothing but foul language and dirty stories, and there's not one other Christian there as far as I can tell."

"I can't pray for you to get a different job," I said. "Why would I pray for God to take the only source of light out of a dark place? That's crazy. Why do you think God leaves us here on earth after we're saved, anyhow?"

"I never thought of it that way," he said. "Do you really think . . . ?"

"Here's what I will do," I said. "I'll join in prayer with you. I want you to call me every morning before you go to work, and we'll pray together that God will help you be light down there."

For two weeks, the man called me and we prayed together every morning. Then he stopped calling. A week later, I saw him and said, "Hey, I'm missing my wake-up call."

"Listen," he said, "since we started praying, three of the guys at work have come to know Christ. I go down early so we can have a Bible study together before work. I don't need to call you, but just keep praying."

"Okay," I said. "Now you'll probably get your new job. God has a core of light there, and I wouldn't be a bit surprised if you got transferred to another place that's just as rotten as this one was when you started."

The life of Christ is incredibly tenacious in a believer, and we need to trust it more. I'm sure someone could tell stories on the other side—how believers were drawn away by evil surroundings. That's where the fellowship of the believers comes in. That's what the collective gathering of the Body is for—to restore and strengthen one another. But that restoration and strengthening is so that we can then go back out as light into the world, not so that we can stay insulated and isolated.

Seeing the Church as Christ's Church

Not only do we fail to trust the life of Christ in other believers, but we also tend to forget whose church it is.

The first year I was in the ministry, I became very frustrated. The church was growing and I was getting the credit, but I knew there was not the slightest relationship between what was happening and what I was doing. I felt utterly useless and completely irrelevant.

The latter part of that year, I landed in the hospital. I was 27 years old, had prepared for the ministry for 9 years and, after less than a year of pastoring, I was in the hospital on a heart machine. Now, there was some question as to whether I could even continue pastoring. My ministry, so-called, had lasted less than 12 months and had been totally ineffective.

As I was lying on one of those dollies they use to wheel people around the hospital, I said, "Lord, I don't understand. I'm still in debt up to my gills for nine years of education. I did what I thought You wanted me to do. But none of it makes any sense."

Then this question came to me: "Jerry, whose church is it?"

I knew the answer to that. I'd been called and ordained. It was my church. That was my answer. Sometimes when I give the Lord a wrong answer, I know right away that it's wrong. Not that God hits me or anything, there's just a divine silence that says, "That was really absurd." This was one of those times.

The Lord miraculously intervened in my life and in my health at that time. He restored my health completely, and I was back in my office in three weeks. There, the question came again: "Whose church is it, Jerry?" A passage from Ephesians 1 came to mind that suddenly brought me alive, for it said that the church "is his body, the fullness of him who fills everything in every way" (v. 23). I had the answer. It was His church, His Body.

Then I went to the Gospels and read Peter's great confession: "You are the Christ, the Son of the living God." Jesus answered, "On this rock [on that confession of God-revealed faith in Him], I will build *my* church, and the gates of Hades will not overcome it" (Matt. 16:16,18, emphasis added).

I saw what had been happening. What I had built, the gates of Hades had overcome. It was gone. But what God had built was still standing. In that moment, I understood that Jesus builds His church and that I not only don't have to build it but also that I cannot build it. That was what had given me trouble. I'd been under the tremendous pressure of having to build a church.

The Lord had been trying to tell me, "It's My church, Jerry. I'll build it."

"Well, Lord, then what am I for?" I said.

"Just hang around and do what I tell you," He said. "Just be available . . . and try to stay out of the way."

Because it's not my church and I don't have to build it, I also don't have to assume a lordship role over the people in it. I can release them to serve Christ. Like me, they simply need to be available to the One who is Lord of the church.

That's all. They don't have to perform. They don't have to
conform, either. And they don't have to become a part of
some organized outreach program.

Releasing the People to Minister

Releasing people to minister means setting them free to
meet other people's needs whenever and however they can.
There doesn't have to be a hook in their ministry that will
get the sinner inside the four walls of their meeting place.

Let's be clear about this: ministering is not inviting people to church services. Inviting people to services is called
"inviting people to services." Ministry is serving people. No
doubt you know people who hate church but need love. Why
would you ever invite such a person to church? What possible sense does it make to invite people who hate church to
come to church? Give them what they need: love, with no
strings attached. If someone is sick, he or she doesn't need
an invitation to church. That person needs a believer to pray
for his or her healing and to give him or her loving care.

I personally feel it's unethical to try to con a person into
church, to make a friend out of someone so that we can
make a convert out of him or her, or to lure a person into
church so we can look good and compete with the church
down the street. We are not in competition with anyone, and
we don't need any underhanded methods that misrepresent
who we are or what we are trying to do.

Every touch we have in the life of another person ought
to be an authentic touch. The reason we try so hard to get people into the church building is because we want to get them
and God together, and we imagine that this is the way to do
it. At least, that is the best reason—at times our motives

aren't that pure. But even when our motives are pure in this regard, our methods and concepts are often wrong. We have been more religious than Christian. Religion, precisely defined, is man's effort to please God. Any human system designed to reach and please any god is properly called a religion. Christianity is not a religion, because its focus is not on man reaching God but on the reverse. God reaches out to man in the person of Jesus Christ.

When we try to get people to God, then, we have things backward. We are being religious instead of being Christian. That, to me, is a profound difference. I call it the "Immanuel Principle." Regarding Jesus' birth, we read, "The virgin will be with child and will give birth to a son, and they will call him Immanuel—which means, 'God with us'" (Matt. 1:23). Jesus was literally Immanuel; He was God with us. He came where we were and brought God to us.

That is Christianity—bringing God to people where they are. That means we don't have to get people someplace; all we need to do is get to them. When we reach out and touch them, God does. That's not egotistical; that's Christian. "God was reconciling the world to himself in Christ" (2 Cor. 5:19). And what did Christ say about us? "As the Father has sent me, I am sending you" (John 20:21). Through the power of the Holy Spirit, we can bring God to people just as Jesus did.

What did Jesus do when He was here? He healed people, many of whom, incidentally, never even thanked Him. He taught people. He loved them. He shared His life with them. He showed them what they could be. He gave them direction. He put up with their failings and patiently showed them a better way. Some people responded to Jesus, and some did not. Those who responded to His touch were saved. And He is working exactly the same way today through His people.

That's exciting, because it means that we don't have to wait for the community to come to church. Many pastors today are trying to get the community into the church. I cannot conceive of that. How would I possibly get a million people into my church? But I can conceive of getting the church into the community. That's a simple matter. Just let the people go, and they will touch every cultural stratum and plant seeds that will produce life. But we must not encourage them to con people or exploit them. Our world has been exploited to death. Everybody wants something, is working an angle, or has a package of goods to sell. Freely we have received from Christ; freely let us give. We need to just give, with no strings attached, and love people where they are. Even if they never come to our church, we need to love them.

Another release we need to give the people of God relates to the way they witness. Pastors have sometimes harangued their people not to be ashamed of Jesus but to tell everyone they meet about Him. I don't believe that Christians are ashamed of Jesus. Those I know are glad to be identified with Him. What sometimes keeps them quiet is not shame but a God-given respect for the rights and integrity of the other person. In situations that are unnerving and unnatural, they don't want to start preaching. And they are absolutely right about that. There is a sense of propriety deep within people, and even in the name of Jesus they don't feel right about violating that propriety. Unfortunately, because of the harangues or other pressures, they sometimes do violate their sense of propriety, and almost always that sort of "witnessing" misfires.

We simply need to be natural and real. If Jesus is a real person in our lives, then others shouldn't have to be around us long before they begin to realize that fact. One way they will know it is because we will be showing God's love toward them, not because we're preaching at them. We must plainly and simply love people.

Then evangelism becomes a serendipity. The word "serendipity" comes from one of Aesop's fables. The three princes of Serendip set out to find, under commission from their king, certain items of enormous wealth and value. While passing through the land seeking these things, they continually find little treasures to take along, although none of these things are what they originally sought. These "incidentals" later prove to be worth more than what they had wanted in the beginning. Any valuable thing we encounter almost unexpectedly along the way is a serendipity.

Evangelism is a serendipity. It just happens along the way for Christians who are living the Immanuel Principle. In my congregation, I can't stop people from coming to Christ now. I don't have to do anything to directly promote evangelism. It just happens.

How do sheep bear lambs? I've never seen a manual written for sheep on how to do this. It wouldn't do a ewe any good even if she could read it. Just get a healthy ewe in the right situation and she'll have a lamb. It will happen naturally. Evangelism is like that. When people learn who they are in Christ and get released to minister, they will minister. It's the most exciting thing in the world.

The Families of the Force

Some time ago, the Lord began to deal with me about a wrong attitude I had. I hesitate to say He *spoke* to me, lest you get the idea that I hear voices. When the Holy Spirit communicates with me, it is seldom, if ever, verbally. Instead, I experience a sudden awareness. It is like a hunch or impression, except that it comes with a unique conviction that marks it as being not of my own invention.

Such an awareness takes much longer to explain than it originally took to understand. Anyhow, in this instance, the insight progressed something like this:

"Jerry, why don't you pastor the whole church?"

"What do You mean, Lord? I thought I was doing a pretty good job."

"Give me the names of 10 kids in your church—the little ones under age 6."

I named my three, and that was it. I suddenly realized that I was not pastoring the children. I didn't know their names. They bothered me. They made noise when I wanted to make noise.

I began to notice how our adults related to the children. When an introduction was made, it would be, "I'm Joe, and this is my wife, Sue." Often a child was standing there, un-introduced and ignored.

I noticed how differently we treated adults. When children ran in the church building, we grabbed them and told them, "Stop it! Be reverent." When adults ran in the church building, we assumed there was an emergency and got out of the way. Is it possible for a child to have an emergency? Double standard.

We were communicating to the children, "You are not important. Christianity is an adult thing." It was that very attitude that prompted Jesus to rebuke His disciples. He told them to let little children come to Him. He taught that the way we treat our children reflects on our relationship with Him, no matter what we may think of our own spiritual brilliance (see Matt. 18:1-6; 19:13-14).

I was heartsick when I realized my error. I didn't love the children. They were a pain in the neck to me. So I asked God to forgive me and to give me love for the children. I began to get down on my knees and talk to them face to face or lift them up to me. I began to ask their names. I also preached a series of messages on offending our children. The Bible says it would be better if we were thrown into the sea with a millstone tied around our neck rather than offend one of these little ones (see Luke 17:2). Isn't that incredible?

The Millstone Around Our Neck

I believe the church of Jesus Christ has often "offended" the little children. Perhaps that is why we often do not enjoy the blessing of God as we could, because there is a millstone around our necks. Our church experienced a new release of life, joy, faith and ministry when we asked God to cut the millstone off our neck and keep us from offending our children.

Our world is terribly unsafe for children. Even parents mistreat their own children. This is clearly the work of Satan, who "comes only to steal and kill and destroy" (John 10:10). But there is more than one way to abuse a child. We who would never batter a child must be careful that we in no way partake of the malevolence of the evil one toward them. We need to reflect the love of Jesus for children.

The Lord really opened my heart to kids. Picture Sally, a little girl with her front teeth missing. She is sitting near the front one morning at a Sunday service. She comes up to me, grabs my hand, pulls me down to her level and says, "Good morning, Pastor. How are you?"

"Fine," I say.

"I want to give you a kiss."

"Okay, give it to me."

She does. I ask her how she's doing and then ask, "Do you love Jesus?"

"Yes," she replies, "and I'm going to serve Jesus all my life."

Then we have a little prayer together.

Sally doesn't have a father. Her mother has been divorced three times, and the girl is less than six years old. I didn't know all that at one time. She was just another kid in the church.

Another kid, Billy, comes up to me and says, "Pastor, when I grow up I want to be a preacher just like you."

"Really?" I ask. "Why?"

"Because I love you."

I believe it is tremendously important that the children be visible in our congregations. I don't mean that they should be allowed to be disruptive, just that they should be seen as part of the church. We need to have times for everyone to get mixed up all together. We must not see the children as the church of tomorrow—they are the church of *right now*. Praise is perfected in the mouth of a child.

This attitude includes teens and pre-teens. So often they almost have their own church. They meet at their own time, have their own service and seldom are involved in the broader life of the entire fellowship. Their pastor is the youth pastor. In one church I'm aware of, the majority of the teens didn't know the name of the senior pastor and knew very few of the other staff members. The youth group was their only world. The rest of the church was for the adults. They never saw the adults, except for their parents (if they attended). And the adults never saw them unless by accident or in passing—just long enough to wonder who those weird looking kids were and what are they doing around there.

Of course, it is important to have youth groups and youth leaders and youth meetings and all the other essentials to ministering to this remarkable generation. But statistics show that these youth-group kids often drop out after high school and never integrate into the broader life of their church. Not only does the Father welcome the praise of children, but also He expects the church to minister to all of them, especially to the many who are hurting and fragmented because of the tragic splintering of their homes and families. This is a ministry a "child" may need even after he or she is grown.

The Big Children

At 22, Debbie was still desperately in need of being loved by a family. Her alcoholic father and her mother had separated when she was small. By fourth grade, she could not respond to affection and had developed an ulcer. By sixth grade, she was an orphan. A grandmother and an uncle raised her after that, but her family took little interest in one another. She had no sense of belonging to a family, much less being a significant part of one.

Even after becoming a Christian, Debbie longed to be part of a regular family. Then it happened. A couple with eight children invited her to come live with them. The result? "Because of my upbringing," Debbie says, "I didn't understand the meaning of words like 'love' and 'forgiveness' and 'acceptance' and 'giving' and 'trust,' but God, through this family, gave life to those words. I have been entirely embraced with my shortcomings and positive qualities alike. How much more then must God accept and embrace me? Now I know—really know—the meaning of those words."

Like Debbie, many other "big children" need the experience of living in a normal family. Runaways, rejected young people, prostitutes, unwed mothers, battered wives—more and more people bear the handicap of a poor family background. A few, like Debbie, have been "adopted" into wholesome Christian families. That's good, and in our church we are encouraging people to do more of it. However, an even greater priority to me is the development of wholesome family relationships in the church. We want to be in the business of preventing situations like Debbie's, not only trying to heal them.

When Love Rules the Home

The environment of the Christian home, like that of the church, should be one of love, acceptance and forgiveness. People need these three things to come to wholeness, and they need them in the home just as much as in the church.

We can have these three ingredients in full measure in our homes only if Jesus Christ is Lord both of the husband and the wife. I am not saying this to put down those who live in divided homes. I don't want anyone to despair. But just as a home is not complete with only a father or mother, neither can love be complete with only one parent being obedient to God.

My purpose is to advocate what God intended the home to be: a place where both husband and wife are under the total Lordship of Jesus Christ. I must warn you that if you are compromising your own commitment to the Lord—if you aren't in the process of becoming what He wants you to be personally—you are heading your home toward disaster. At our church, people come to us with incredible marriage and family disasters. They come from every walk of life, from high income and low income and everything in between. Usually the disaster is a result of the husband or wife (or both) not being committed to Christ.

If Jesus isn't your Lord, you must begin there to bring love, acceptance and forgiveness into your home. In Romans 5:5, Paul says, "God has *poured* out his love [*agape*] into our hearts." How? "By the Holy Spirit." If Jesus Christ is not your Lord—if the Holy Spirit is not filling your life—you do not have *agape* love. Sure, you can fake it. You can have friendship, and you can have emotional love. But just as you can't buy apples at an auto parts store, you can't get *agape* anywhere but from God. He is the exclusive source.

Agape love must become the mark of our homes. "Husbands, love your wives, just as Christ loved the church and gave himself up for her" (Eph. 5:25). There it is again, *agape* joined with giving. *Agape* is always a giving love.

Do you know what an ideal marriage is? It is husband and wife each giving to the other all of the time. If both are giving, obviously both are getting as well, but the dynamic is completely different. I know a relationship is in trouble whenever a husband or wife says to me, "I am not getting anything out of this marriage." It is right to expect something from the marriage relationship, but it is not right for a person to get married for what he or she can get out of it.

"This marriage just isn't fulfilling," a husband once complained to me. "Who said it was supposed to be?" I asked. "Is your fulfillment your wife's responsibility?" He seemed baffled at the question, as are many people. We must not give our fulfillment away to anyone else. To have a fulfilling, happy life is our responsibility. Too often we are looking to our jobs, our marriages, our hobbies or our accomplishments to give us fulfillment. They won't. They can't. Fulfillment has to do with completeness, the sense of wholeness, and that comes from only one source.

In Colossians 2:9-10, Paul writes, "For in Him dwells all the fullness of the Godhead bodily; and you are complete in Him" (*NKJV*). When you find your completeness in Him, you then are able to bring a fulfilled person to your marriage. You can bring a happy person to your relationship. That changes a lot of things. Most of all, it makes it possible for you to really love the other person rather than love yourself through them.

Love gives, and it gives with the idea of meeting the other person's needs—emotional and spiritual as well as physical. One of the greatest love gifts you can give your partner in marriage is total, unqualified *acceptance*. You see, although I speak of love, acceptance and forgiveness as three distinct things, they are closely related.

It comes as something of a shock to most of us when we discover we didn't marry a saint after all. We married a sinner like ourselves. Acceptance means we give each other enough elbow room to live. Acceptance conveys the idea that "you don't have to be my ideal. I love you." This is real unqualified acceptance as the person now is and does not imply, "I will accept you in spite of your obvious faults." That idea is egotistical.

Too often, we act in such a way as to communicate, "You are not exactly what I would like you to be." We compare here, suggest there, manipulate elsewhere, con a little, play little reward games. Why? We are not the Lord, and no one has to answer to us, including our spouses.

If you have a very capable husband or wife, beware of getting into competition. I was intimidated by my wife's grade point average when we were in college ages ago. Barbara was always disciplined, got her assignments in on time, made *A*s on the tests. I was always playing ping-pong or softball or basketball, drinking cokes and running around. I could never figure out why she had a better GPA than I did. I was intimidated by her grades, and I was intimidated by her discipline.

Years later, she launched her "Touch of Beauty" radio broadcasts. Way down inside of me, there lurked a subtle fear that she would do better than me. Sure enough, that which I feared came true. Men would come up and say, "We listen to your wife every day on the radio." Competition.

God helped me realize that Barbara and me are not in competition and that we can release one another to be what God wants each of us to be. I am not threatened now. I accept her strengths, and they don't intimidate me any longer. I also accept her weaknesses, and she does the same for me.

The greatest gift you can ever give your spouse is to accept him or her. I call it "the gift of significance." If you have trouble with this, perhaps it is because at some subtle point you have not been able to accept yourself. In turn, that may be because you are not thoroughly convinced that God accepts you.

I lived a lot of my life trying to get God to accept me. I didn't like me very well. I was too short. My ears were too big. I wasn't put together the way I thought best.

I was crossing the street in Seattle one day when the Lord spoke to me clearly and said, "Jerry, why don't you quit trying to be a Christian? You are one. You are accepted in the beloved." I did not even know that last phrase was in the Bible.

Three days later, I was lying on my bed in the room I was renting near my university. I opened my Bible to Ephesians 1 and began reading. When I reached the sixth verse, it jumped on me like a thing alive: I am "accepted in the beloved" (*KJV*).

That experience totally changed my life. Suddenly, I realized I didn't have to get God to like me anymore. He had liked me all the time. As I began to accept myself because God accepted me, I found I was better able to accept other people. So acceptance, like love, depends on a right relationship with God that includes exercising the faith to believe that God loves and accepts us in Christ.

Forgiveness in the Home

Along with love and acceptance, forgiveness is one of the most healing elements in a home or church. Now, forgiveness involves releasing. We have not truly forgiven someone until that matter is dismissed by us, not to be retained anymore. I don't mean that we forget it in terms of memory. I mean we don't hold on to it. People tend to retain grievances, and although they "forgive," they keep things in a little bag for instant recall as needed. Introduce that system into a home, and it becomes absolutely devastating. One cannot live with a person who is collecting another's mistakes in a little bundle and bringing them up periodically just to show that person that he or she is not nearly as smart as he or she thinks, because remember when . . .

"There we go again. I thought that was settled."

"Well, it is, but . . ."

When people live together in the same home, their weaknesses are going to show. They just will. A strong relationship is not one in which the people have no weaknesses but one in which each person knows how to handle in love the other's failings.

Married couples so often get into little ego struggles. A minor issue—leaving a rake in the yard, being late for an appointment, not putting gas in the car—becomes a major issue. Then it becomes a matter of, "You're always doing something stupid or irresponsible." We generalize from a small issue into a great accusation and get caught in an ego struggle. The classic example is the huge, enormous problem that arises when the husband squeezes the toothpaste tube in the middle and the wife rolls it from the end. All they would need to do is buy two tubes of toothpaste, let him squeeze all he wants and her roll to her heart's content. That would take care of it.

Such conflicts can be funny to hear about but hurt when you are caught in one. Multiply the hurt by many repetitions and many other small issues, and you come up with two people who love each other but have lost each other.

They no longer communicate. Many such couples find each other only in their children. That is their one meeting point. When those children are gone, the husband and wife separate or spend the rest of their lives together but alienated.

Couples can build an environment in which they will not lose each other if they let love and acceptance rule the home and learn a few things about forgiveness. "Bear with each other and forgive whatever grievances you may have against one another. Forgive as the Lord forgave you" (Col. 3:13). Has Christ forgiven you? Then that is your basis for forgiving others. As a Christian, you have no excuse to be unforgiving in any relationship, particularly in your home. Forgive.

I must emphasize the importance of forgiveness not just as an event but also as an environment, a lifestyle.

"I forgave him for that thing."

Not good enough. You must forgive him for everything, all the time. People need the security of knowing they can blow it and still be loved and totally forgiven with nothing held over their heads. I am pleading for an environment of forgiveness in our homes, where people don't have to wonder or endure some painful interlude before they can be forgiven.

That is the kind of home I need. Not that I intend to offend. I am not asking for license. I am not asking to be a tyrant and still be loved. I don't want to be unreasonable. I don't want to be hard to live with. Not many men do, though it may look that way.

Sometimes, I meet a husband who seems to want to be hard to live with. I think, *He must be trying to be ornery, because he is certainly succeeding.* When I get close to him, however, I find a frustrated person who can't understand why there is trouble and why people have a hard time with him. I don't know any woman who tries to be contentious either.

I know several who have succeeded, but none who planned it that way.

We need to build an environment in which husbands and wives understand that their mates are not holding grudges against them or remembering the mistakes of the past. In my own life, I need to know that when my wife looks at me, she's not screening me through all of the foolish things I have done over the past 47 years. I've done a few, but I honestly think she has forgotten most of them. Or at least she has convinced me she has, which is just as good. She doesn't throw the past up to me, and I try not to throw the past up to her.

Forgiveness is liberating. If we don't have an environment of forgiveness, we can't live freely. We can only defend ourselves constantly. What chance do we have then? None whatsoever, because we are all going to fail sometimes.

I've seen husbands and wives live together as though they were vultures. He's perched over here and she's perched over there, and they meet in an arena between. Each is just waiting for the other to make a mistake so he or she can lash out. Have you learned yet that people tend to live up to your expectations of them? Just perch there watching for your husband or wife to blow it again and you probably won't have to wait too long.

"My husband is never on time for anything," a woman said to me. "And he is always in a bad mood. He has never been able to handle money, either." She went down a list of about 15 things her husband "always" or "never" did.

When she finished, I said, "You undoubtedly have the most consistent husband I've ever heard of. You have been married for 24 years, and this guy has made totally wrong decisions all that time. Quite a record."

You get the point, and so did she. What are you looking for? You will find it. If you are looking for a mistake you will find it, but forgiveness does not look for mistakes. When the mistake is there anyhow, it forgives. This paves the way for continued healthy living. Unforgiveness becomes a gate across your road of life. It drops down and you can't get through to go on. Only forgiveness can open that gate.

If you want a good home, build an environment that grows good homes. How do you have a good garden? Pull out the weeds and plant good seeds, not bad ones. If you are planting seeds of rebellion, jealousy, suspicion, unforgiveness and criticism, what are you going to grow? You will reap what you sow. To have a home in which love reigns, sow seeds of love. How do you do that? By being a loving person. You can be a loving person when Jesus Christ is Lord of your life and the Holy Spirit is shedding abroad the love of God in your heart.

What I'm saying about husbands and wives applies to parents and children as well. I know parents who are unforgiving toward their children. They remember every mistake that kid ever made. Parents whose children are grown and married tell me about the mistakes those kids made when they were still at home.

Forgive your children. Forgive that teenager.

"But he hurt me."

Forgive it and release it. Let the wound heal.

I'd like to inject into your home these three things—love, acceptance and forgiveness—but I can't. All I can do is point you to Jesus. He loves you, accepts you and forgives you. As you are exposed to His love, you can begin to love. As you realize His acceptance, you can begin to accept others. As you experience His forgiveness, you can forgive.

How many of your past sins does God remember? None whatsoever. There is no record of you in heaven as a sinner. As far as God is concerned, your life began when Jesus became your Lord. Bless God. That's strong. That's forgiveness. Put it to work in your home.

Learning the Christian Lifestyle at Home

I am utterly convinced that most churches have not done a good job of teaching children the Word of God. We have taught them information, but we have not taught them lifestyle. The evidence of that is in the many sinners who know the Bible. They grew up in our Sunday Schools and children's ministries, but they are living for the devil. They know the answers, but they don't follow the Lord. They have the information, but not the lifestyle.

Some time ago, I decided that I was through educating people to go out and be more knowledgeable sinners. It was simply impossible to go on that way. I didn't know how my church and I could better teach lifestyle, but we began to search for a way. We looked all over the country, in vain, for churches that had resolved this dilemma. Few were even asking the same question in any urgent way. What could we do?

We went to the Bible and asked, *What principles can we find in Scripture, and how can we implement those principles in a church of 3,000 or 4,000?* We knew we faced an incredible task, but it had to be done. The first thing that became clear from the Scriptures is that home is the place and parents are the people when it comes to providing Christian nurture. The Old Testament established it, and the New Testament affirmed it (see Deut. 6:6-7; Eph. 6:4).

Our church's mentality, like that of many others, had been, "Families, support your local children's ministry." I agree that in most cases families should do this, but we began to see the distortion in this concept. Children's ministries should actually support the family. The church has been allowed to usurp the place of the home as an institution for the spiritual training of children. When that proves inadequate, we turn to the Christian day school. But that doesn't work either.

We have forgotten that children learn their values and their lifestyle at home. So the church must focus on the family as a unit. The family must not only become healthy in its environment but also effective in its communication of Christian truth.

With these principles in mind, East Hill developed and launched a pilot program called "Home Base."[1] Mike Harris developed it. Rick Boes, who initially coordinated the program, explained, "With programs in the past, parents sat back and let the church take responsibility for teaching their children. Home Base runs directly counter to that, in that parents are taught to teach Christian principles at home. In addition, Home Base gets families together to share ideas. In this way, strong families can help weak ones." It also works the other way around, because we can all learn from one another when it comes to ways of communicating Christian truth in everyday family living.

When we introduced the Home Base program, it did not mean that we abandoned formal Christian education programs in our church. In fact, we wanted every member, each week, to have one corporate worship experience, one family learning experience, and one peer group experience. Home Base provided the family learning experience.

Many of the relationships established between families in that program 30 years ago are still strong today, and more than a few of the children of those families are now married to each other and establishing their own Christian homes. But we live in a world of radically fractured families, even within the church fellowship. Today, it is fortunate for a child to just have both a mom and a dad, let alone a Christian home to grow up in.

We did a couple of things that helped. We continued a quality children's ministry from nursery through grade six. As much as possible, we had each class taught by both a husband and wife. This not only gave a wonderful expression of ministry for the couples but also provided a model for the kids of a Christian mom and dad working together with love and respect. In the summers, we sponsored elaborate children's Bible Schools in the local parks. These also involved husband and wife teams. Many of our couples would take a week of their vacations to work in these events.

When our junior high and high school ministries became so large that we could no longer maintain a personal touch with each one, we had healthy husbands and wives serve as advisors for the teens in groups of 6 to 10. Our college and single adult ministry had a Sunday-night-after-church event in which one of our church families would host a group for a general time of singing, fellowship and snacks. The group brought all the food and did all the serving and cleanup, while the host couple shared how they had come to follow Christ and told something about their home. We were looking for models for these young people, many of whom had never seen a working Christian home.

Whatever we do, we must do everything we can to build healthy Christian homes and then return Christian education to that home. Where that is not possible, we must bring godly models—not just biblical information—to the children and teens of our congregations.

Our Own Families First

In our church, we do not appeal to families to support the church and its programs. Instead, we try to develop ways to support the family. We believe the family unit is central in God's plan.

Now, it would not be consistent of us to take the position I just stated and then ask the leaders of our church to sacrifice their own family life for the sake of the "work of the Lord." So if a staff member comes to me with a family problem, I say, "What do you need? Do you need time away? Do you need to go walk on the beach with your wife? What? Anything you need, we'll help." Then I send the staff member home and say that I don't want to see him or her back in the office until things are okay at home.

The elders in our fellowship are volunteers who carry a specific and vigorous ministry load. They pray with people and serve communion at every meeting of the church as well as minister to the sick or those who need help during the week. They also serve as a spiritual advisory board to me. Not long ago, an elder came to me and said that his children were getting hard to control. His wife was getting edgy, and he was troubled about his family. I asked him how much time he thought he needed to take care of the problem, and he said six months. I told him to take a year and get things under control at home. If things were okay before that time, that would be fine, but he had a year free from any duties. All the other elders prayed with him and blessed him. I am glad to report that he took the steps that were needed to get his family back to health. He returned within the year to a place of ministry.

My own family is extremely important to me, and I take Mondays each week to be with them. I am never available for anything else on Mondays, no matter what it is. If you come to my house and knock on the door on a Monday, I will not answer it. I don't answer my phone. Only my secretary can reach me at an unlisted number, and that only in the most extreme circumstances.

I also set aside certain evenings for my family. Nothing violates that. Pressures of church business are never allowed to intrude. One important event is the shopping sprees I have with my daughters. I do all of the school and special-occasion clothes shopping with them. Spending all day at the mall gives us wonderful one-on-one time with each other. Both of my daughters are grown women now, but every once in a while they still want "a shopping spree with Dad." I considered that an act of love not only to God and my family but also to the congregation, as I would have no ministry left if my home were to disintegrate.

It's not that our church just decided to emphasize the family throughout the life of our congregation. We didn't make that decision. God did. We're simply trying to listen to Him.

Note

1. Over the years, readers have often asked me about this program. The developer of the program was Michael Harris, who is now teaching others how to teach children. He works primarily in the Sudan. He can be contacted at michaelcharris@gmail.com.

DEALING WITH DIFFICULTIES

Have you found that you don't change easily? Many people change only under pressure. Not because they want to, but because they must. Nothing in human experience is a greater catalyst for change than pressure—usually the pressure of some sort of difficulty. Yet we ordinarily do all we can to avoid pressure situations. Non-pressured living has become almost a god in our world. It is also a myth.

If you design a life free of pressures, you probably also will have a life of mediocrity. Count on it: without pressure there is little change, and without change there can be no growth. As Dr. James D. Mallory puts it, "People seem to assume that conflict is inherently bad or that the ideal life would be one that is conflict free. Anybody that is conflict free, I would suspect, is not experiencing growth. . . . The important changes in us take place within the framework of struggle."[1]

Another James put it this way: "Is your life full of difficulties and temptations? Then be happy, for when the way is rough, your patience has a chance to grow. So let it grow, and don't try to squirm out of your problems. For when your patience is finally in full bloom, then you will be ready for anything, strong in character, full and complete" (Jas. 1:2-4, *TLB*).

Welcoming difficulties in the life of the church isn't easy. Yet every difficulty that arises also presents an opportunity for growth, either for individual members or for the corporate body. The church's difficulties are either problems with people (the resolution of which should lead to personal growth) or problems with practice (the resolution of which should lead to corporate growth).

Problems with people tend to revolve around certain personality traits. Let's consider a few examples.

Criticism

Nothing can tear up a fellowship quicker than the spread of criticism, and nothing is more antipathetic to love, acceptance and forgiveness. The two attitudes cannot coexist.

I was once away from the congregation for about three weeks to hold a pastors conference in New Zealand. When I left home, the people at East Hill were concerned with loving one another and being filled with the Holy Spirit. I returned to find them upset, unhappy and jabbing at one another.

The women's ministry had sponsored a fashion show. As a part of the show, one of the women had modeled a bikini. The local newspaper covered the fashion show and, along with the article, ran one picture. You guessed it—a shot of the gal in the bikini. Some of our members were quite upset about this turn of events and were ripping into the model and the women responsible for the fashion show.

The bikini had been only a small part (no pun intended) of the fashion show, which in turn was only a part of the program that night. In fact, through the testimonies and the entire program, several of the 500-plus women in attendance gave their lives to Christ. The newspaper had presented a positive write-up of the show, praising it as one of the finest they had seen. And the bikini photo had been published without comment.

When all this landed in my lap on my return from New Zealand, I was upset. Not about the bikini—it's ludicrous to be upset about a bikini in a fashion show for women only and not about the ones being worn at almost every public swimming pool. Anyhow, only women were present, and it would not have mattered to me if they had been modeling lingerie. I could see some reason for concern over the picture in the paper, but I was a whole lot more concerned that Christians were ripping other Christians and that a spirit of criticism was replacing a spirit of love, acceptance and forgiveness.

I met privately with the woman who had modeled the bikini and the woman who had set up the fashion show. I said, "There has been some objection to the content, as you know. Most of the complaints have come from men, none of whom were present. Perhaps they have a small point; maybe you need to evaluate your program. But no one is judging you. I'm backing you 100 percent, and that is what I'm telling those who come to me."[2] The women decided they would forego their rights and omit bikinis in the future. It was no big deal.

The more serious problem, the unloving criticism, called for action from me. I brought the whole situation out in the open in a service. I told the people that according to 1 Corinthians 8:1, knowledge (in this case, knowledge of what should not be done and why) puffs up but love builds up. I told them that they were responding to this situation below the level of their maturity in Christ. Love won the day, the critics saw their error, and the fellowship was restored.

If the women had actually done something wrong, I would still have taken action against any critical spirit I saw developing in the congregation. If something is wrong, we must simply acknowledge that it is wrong and pray that the devil won't be able to seize on it as a means of hurting people. We don't empower the devil's work by making or promoting attacks on the people involved. We talk with them, deal with the issue, and treat them with love, acceptance and forgiveness.

Quick to Take Offense

Sometimes people get offended with one another or the pastor. These situations must be resolved immediately before they get worse. Often, the problem is spiritual in origin. The Bible says, "Great peace have they which love thy law: and nothing shall offend them" (Ps. 119:165, *KJV*). A person who is easily offended apparently doesn't love God's law very much.

Unresolved offenses tend to harden into bitterness and spread to other people. Thus, individual believers who are offended should take steps to resolve the matter themselves. As Hebrews 12:14-15 states, "Make every effort to live in peace with all men and to be holy; without holiness no one will see the Lord. See to it that no one misses the grace of God and that no bitter root grows up to cause trouble and defile many." In the last analysis, those who have been offended must deal with the problem themselves, because if they choose to be offended, no solution imposed or appeal from others can mollify them. As Scripture says, "An offended brother is more unyielding than a fortified city, and disputes are like the barred gates of a citadel" (Prov. 18:19).

About all we can do with people who are offended is appeal to them. I recall a situation which arose among our staff members. Three secretaries got upset with one another, and the staff pastor with whom they worked was out of town. So it fell to me to do something. I called the three of them into my office and told them that I was embarrassed to have to talk to people we had hired about this sort of thing. I said, "I don't care who is right or wrong. I don't want to know any details. This is not a trial, so you don't need to present your case. I only know that you are not relating as sisters in Christ. I'm going to leave the room. There's a half hour left in the day for you to get this thing ironed out. I want you to come out of here loving each other. I want you to pray with one another. I want you to forgive one another. I want each of you to call me tonight and tell me that is exactly what you have done." Then I left and went golfing.

They all called me that night. As I had hoped, they had gotten matters straightened out, and everything was right again. Praise God! Let's help one another to see that we are bigger people than to indulge in that kind of nonsense. Let's keep our relationships right, and then the right and wrong of issues that arise will work out.

I could have held court, attempting to judge right and wrong, but even if I had succeeded in that, these women still would not have liked one another. What good would I have done?

A woman in our congregation became offended at me because I didn't visit her in the hospital while she was ill. She had been there seven days and was complaining to various people that "nobody" visited her. However, when we checked into it, we discovered she had an average of four people a day visit her—28 visits in 7 days from people in the church.

I called her at home and asked how she was feeling. "Well, I'm feeling fine . . . *now,*" she said.

"I understand you've been in the hospital," I said.

"Well," she said, "it's a little bit late."

"A little late for what?"

"I was there for seven days, and nobody even came to visit."

I told her that I understood she had visitors from the church every day. "Yes," she said, "people from the church came, but you didn't come."

I said I knew that, but I figured all the other people who came to see her had the power of Jesus too, and that every person who walked into her room represented a visit from Jesus. Was it possible she had missed all those visits from Him because she was hung up on the personality of one man? I wanted her to see Jesus in her brothers and sisters, whether the pastor got there or not.

She said she had never looked at it quite like that, but she got the point. And she quit being offended.

Debate with Schismatics

"Avoid foolish controversies and genealogies and arguments and quarrels about the law, because these are unprofitable and useless. Warn a divisive person once, and then warn him a second time. After that, have nothing to do with him. You may be sure that such a man is warped and sinful; he is self-condemned" (Titus 3:9-11).

We are not to enter into debate with schismatics. It's not that there is no room for people of good faith to discuss or even disagree on issues, but if a person is habitually gendering strife (see 2 Tim. 2:23), causing confusion and creating division, he or she must not be allowed to continue.

You can identify schismatics by the backwash in people's lives. They touch one person, and that person becomes confused. They touch someone else, and that one is angry with this one. In their wake, schismatics leave all kinds of confusion and strife. Another word for the schismatic is "troublemaker."

Sometimes these people are not aware of what they are doing. They don't realize the effect they are having on others. That's why Scripture says to warn them once and then a second time. I once had to go that far in dealing with a troublemaker. In our second conversation, I said, "One of two things can happen now: you can stop it, or you can leave. You must decide whether your fellowship in this Body is of enough value to you to stop what you are doing and begin to relate rightly. You decide and I'll call you to learn what your decision is." The person to whom I said this responded well. He really needed to get some things straightened out in his life. I referred him to a counselor who worked through his problems with him, and eventually he found healing.

When I give a teaching, I don't demand that everyone agree with me. But I do demand that no one sows discord in the Body by campaigning for an opposing view. Suppose, for example, that one of the teachers in the congregation began to present some views that ran counter to what I was preaching from the platform. That teacher and I would have a conversation the very same week. If I detected a sincere desire in that teacher to get the truth across, we would discuss how to do that together. I would ask for his views, and we would together seek a proper balance in our preaching and teaching. And we would set down certain policies governing our relationship. We would commit ourselves to support one another.

But if I detected rebellion in that teacher, I would confront it, for he or she would be playing the role of a schismatic. One's attitude and motive is the issue. You can't work with a person who is "warped and sinful" and who won't repent.

The Traditionalist

When church-as-a-force principles are put into practice, some people become uncomfortable. They are used to the old ways, and things don't seem quite right to them. We need to treat these people with understanding. It's one thing to shatter old traditions, but quite another to shatter people. When we feel we need to do the first, we must be careful not to do the second in the process.

People come into our congregation because the life of the church appeals to them and draws them. But after being with us awhile, they begin looking around for some of the things they were accustomed to seeing in other fellowships. One woman came to me and said, "Pastor, do you have a visitation program here in this church?"

I knew exactly what was happening. She was beginning to look around to see if we had the elements traditionally considered necessary to a live church. I said, "We certainly do. We have what is probably one of the best visitation programs of any church in the world."

"You do? Really?" she said.

I just knew the next step would be for her to draw from her purse a list of names of people the visitation committee should call on, so I paused only a moment.

"Yes, we do," I said, "and you're it."

"What?" she said.

"You're it," I said. "You are the visitation committee." It turned out that she did have a list of names. I told her that if people who needed a visit came to her attention, they were automatically her assignment. We save a lot of lost motion by not channeling everything through a committee. Our visitation program has the simplest structure in the world: you see the need, you meet it.

People simply need to be instructed. Otherwise, they become confused. They don't understand, and they misinterpret what they see happening or not happening. In our church, a core of people who know what the church as a force is all about communicate the principles to newer people as the need arises. We also have training sessions for new members, which also helps.

In addition to all kinds of problems that arise because of difficulties with people, every church faces problems because of difficulties with practice. One of the most common and most troublesome of such difficulties concerns the role of the pastor.

What Is a Pastor to Do?

I believe pastors need to focus their ministry where their strength is. That is, they need to operate in the area of their gifts and calling. Most pastors, unlike Jesus, do not do all things well. This causes all sorts of complications.

Many churches play a variation of musical chairs with their pastors. Suppose a church has a pastor who is good at personal counseling and gives his or her energies to it. As a result, the preaching ministry is neglected. When the time comes to call a new pastor, the pressure is on to find a person who is strong in the pulpit. Sure enough, the next pastor preaches well but is not a good administrator or is not good at one-to-one relationships with people.

How can a church provide a balanced ministry to the community with a pastor whose gifts and calling are limited? If a pastor of limited abilities (and that's about all of us) pursues his or her specialty and lets other needed work go undone, the church will be out of balance. If the pastor tries to do everything, he will come out frustrated. Even the work the pastor could have done well suffers because he is drained emotionally by trying to perform those tasks that he cannot do well.

The only answer that seems to make sense is to enlist more than one person to do the many tasks that all too often fall to the pastor alone. A person's gifts and calling may be narrow, but he or she can still perform a wide range of functions. And in a smaller church, the pastor almost has to do that. But he should be working all the time toward giving away everything that is peripheral to his own personal calling.

As a congregation grows, staff may have to be added, though it is my belief that most churches are radically overstaffed. When overstaffing happens, policies begin to take over to compensate for direct communication. The church organization then begins to feel and look like any other institution with its professional staff and paper shuffling. If additional staff becomes absolutely necessary, the aim must be to release the pastor to his personal calling.

As our church grew, I had to make a basic choice. Was I called to counsel, to administrate, to communicate truth in the public teaching ministry, or what? My calling was to teach. So, when the load became too much and a person needed care beyond the abilities of normal friendship, we were able to add a staff member whose strength was personal care and, eventually, an administrator. As they added their strengths to mine, the needs of the church were more fully met and each of us was happier and more effective.

"Well," you might say, "that's great if you have a lot of money and can afford it. But we are new and still small, and we can't afford it. Then what?"

This is an important question, but it reflects institutional thinking—the idea that professionals must do the ministry. In a church as a force, the leadership sees the gifts and strengths of those whom they are leading. As our church grew, I found there were many people in our congregation who were excellent administrators at their jobs. They were more than willing to help in those areas.

Much of the counseling I did was just giving a sensitive listening ear and meaningful prayer. There were those in our fellowship who were gifted in that area. I might have had the first meeting with the couple who needed help and then introduced them to a couple who had a healthy marriage. That couple was delighted to carry on the conversation and become caring friends to the person. If the issue was more serious and professional help was needed, I would refer them to a trusted Christian psychologist and be their pastor through the process. I am a pastor, not a professional psychologist or counselor. I have to know my own limitations and stay stubbornly within them. People will often expect more than what you can deliver. Be sure of where your limits are and respect them.

It is amazing how many personal issues can be handled through a loving, sensitive friendship. I always had people in my pocket. That is, I had people whom I had talked to earlier and explained what I was doing. They knew that whenever I brought someone and introduced him or her, it was not just a social call. I was giving them a ministry assignment. I was then available to them to answer questions or give needed help. This continues to be my practice today. Even when our church numbered in the thousands, I still had my pockets full of people who would enter into a caring relationship with a hurting person.

When a church does begin to hire staff, the pastor's calling must always be kept in mind. The church can't just go out and hire an "associate pastor." The church will do better and the pastor will live longer when the person is mated to the task. I can preach three times on a Sunday morning and not be tired at all. I enjoy teaching seminars, and I can go home from teaching one stronger than when I left. But let me counsel for a few hours and I'm worn out. It exhausts me. We have a man who can sit in his office for seven days a week and counsel people. He can have appointments all day long and still come out strong. He can't understand how I'm able to preach several times a day, and I can't understand how he can counsel all day, every day.

Administration is the same way. I am impatient with details. I dream big dreams, set directions and make far-reaching decisions. It may take a whole department six months to work out all the details connected with implementing one basic decision. I can't handle that. If I had to herd all those details through the endless meetings required, I would go crazy.

Our administrator can come out of one of those sessions and say to me, "Boy, we had a good business meeting." I'll say to him, "There is no such thing!" He comes out excited; I'm worn to a frazzle. That is why he is the administrator. That is his strength. He enjoys working out the details that transform a dream into a reality. Administrative people are responders, not directors. They take direction and then make things happen.

Now, on the other hand, if I were an administrator and the pastor of the church, I would seek to add staff in the area of Bible teaching and counseling. If I were a counselor, I would add administrative and teaching staff. Visitation? I don't see that as a staff function. Neither is evangelism. Those are the people's ministries.

What Kind of Building Do We Need?

The question just considered, "What is a pastor to do?" was answered in part by the principles of the church as a force. The pastor is not to do the people's ministry for them. Church-as-a-force principles can also tell you a lot about what sort of building you will need.

Do you have the church-as-a-force concept well enough in mind yet to anticipate what I am going to say as to the first decision you need to make regarding facilities? It's simple. Before you can decide what kind of building you need, you must decide whether you need one at all.

"Oh, but of course a church must have a building." Really? Where is it written in Scripture? I've been studying my Bible intensively for years, and I still cannot find either a design for a church building or any statement that we should have one. Before you can decide whether or not you need a building, you must know specifically why your church is in existence. What is your unique ministry to your community? Are you just there to be redundant?

What good are you if you are simply going to duplicate what some other church is already doing in the community? For example, if another church in your area having great success with a Christian school, kindergarten through grade 12, there is no reason for you to rush in with a similar, competing program. In fact, it's good reason not to do so. Obviously, whether or not your calling is to operate a school has a great bearing on what facilities you need to build.

Don't automatically assume that you need to build anything. Perhaps your church should meet in homes, at a public school, in the armory, in a rented hall, at someone else's church building. Your own ill-conceived building could turn out to be a tremendous liability, locking you into a situation that will hinder rather than help you in accomplishing what God has in mind for you.

Suppose you do need to build. The first thing to remember is that you are not building a church but rather a place for the church to meet. The church is people, and the building must be constructed in such a way that it will serve the people. Don't allow a reversal of that in which the church becomes servant to the building. In other words, don't let the building limit you from doing what you want to do. Make sure it is functional and serves all your purposes. Because the church is people, you need to design a people-centered building. When people walk in, they should sense the importance of people and not be overcome by a huge cross, window, chandelier or whatever.

When you apply the church-as-a-force concept to building, you can save money by deleting unnecessary and sometimes undesirable extras. How many things in the average church building are there simply because it's a church? Because the church is not the building, you can be free from all of that.

When people walk into your church, the first thing they should see is another person. Their eyes should not be drawn to the ceiling, the window, the platform or anywhere else. They should be able to look at someone who will look right back at them, who will welcome them with a spirit of love and acceptance. Then they can begin to understand at once what the church really is.

In the worship service, people need to see each other because they are worshiping together. They haven't come as spectators to watch the performers on the platform. The seating should be arranged in some semicircular pattern so that the people will not have to look only at the backs of other people's heads. Because they haven't come to watch a superstar, the platform area should be simple and designed to bring the pastor close to the people. The sound system must also be mobile so that people can have the capability of participating from their places throughout the sanctuary.

In summary, if you need to build, spend sufficient time first in determining the features you need in order to accomplish your ministry. Then get professional people to tell you how to do it. Don't get some lone-duck contractor with a cheap idea of what a church should be. Get someone who knows what he or she is doing and can do it right. It will pay in the long run.

How Can a Big Church Stay Person-Centered?

I once believed that a congregation of about 300 persons was ideal. I thought a big church could not possibly meet the needs of its members and that whenever a church threatened to become too large, it should branch out and start another church. Obviously, I don't feel that way anymore. Today I think that a church of 3,000 is not too large, nor is a church of 30,000 too large. I mean that, so let me explain why I feel that way.

When Peter preached on the Day of Pentecost, 3,000 people were converted then and there (see Acts 2:41). These people "devoted themselves to the apostles' teaching and to the fellowship, to the breaking of bread and to prayer" (v. 42). In other words, there were more than 3,000 members in the church at Jerusalem in its beginning. The principles of church life were originally formed in and are designed for a congregation of thousands. And it is in a church of thousands that these principles may be expected to work best.

This is a concept we need to grasp, because so many times we have a mental block about size. I had a tremendous barrier in my own mind in this regard. I simply could not believe that church life could be increased in its effectiveness, enjoyment and value to the individual as the numbers multiplied. But I found out it can.

When church life suffers in quality as the numbers increase, it is because the church has not adhered to New Testament principles—the concepts of the church as a force, if you will. The church as a force is person-centered. If the big church stays person-centered, it will increase its effectiveness with its size. If it ceases to be person-centered, it will begin to die from within.

The big danger that confronts a growing church is institutionalism. Organizations are forever trying to usurp the place of people. They try to minister by committee. They structure and control and direct and swallow up people. Institutionalism is so subtle and so pervasive that it creeps in without us ever realizing it. If we aren't watchful, the institution will continue to swell and the people will start to shrink, as far as church life is concerned.

One reason we get sucked into institutionalism is that
we want predictability. Institutions are safe. They are man-
ageable. They are the same today as they were yesterday. We
know where to plug in and we know where to unplug. We
like that sort of security. But it is deadly when we get caught
up in a machine and forget that God's church is first, last
and always people. Churches do not exist for the sake of the
machine. They are not cogs in something bigger and more
important than the individual.

East Hill has a benevolence ministry. We give food and
clothing to those who are in need. As a part of this ministry,
we operated a 17-acre collective farm. Our people marked it
off in plots, grew gardens and supplied individuals as well as
various social agencies with food. We provided hundreds of
pounds of potatoes as well as other vegetables in this way. It
was beautiful.

The man who coordinated this effort came to one of our
council meetings to request a doubling of funds for the program. His request was legitimate, and he showed just how
the funds would be used. But somehow, something didn't
seem right to me. I sensed a hesitation within, and I said,
"Wait, something is not right here. We need to table this for
a while and think about it."

What was wrong? Only one thing: we were beginning to
institutionalize. We were getting everything centralized so
that anyone who had goods to give put it in a pot. Then
those who had needs were directed to the pot. We were training our people to say to a needy person, "Go on down to the
benevolence office, they'll take care of you." This would re-
place, "Oh, you need help; I'd like to do something. We have
some extra food. I have some clothes for your children,
clothes my little ones have outgrown."

Although we were acting from the best of motives, we were taking ministry away from the people and institutionalizing it. And it was happening without us even realizing it. So we denied the budget increase. I went to the congregation, told them about it, and said, "Now you are the benevolence department of this church. The garden plots are yours to continue growing things. But it is up to you to order your lives so that you have resources available to meet people's needs."

True, our members couldn't get a tax break doing it that way. It wouldn't show on their tithing record. But so what? It is what we give in secret without thought of reward or recognition that most pleases God.

Difficulties—they never quit coming. By their very nature, they are no fun. But they don't have to trouble us unduly either. We don't have to become cynics, murmuring, grumbling, feeling sorry for ourselves and asking mournfully, "What next?" If we have a solid philosophical base in the principles of the church as a force, we can deal with difficulties and come out stronger in the process.

Notes

1. James D. Mallory and Stanley Baldwin, *The Kink and I* (Wheaton, IL: Victor Books, 1973). Used by permission.
2. As I read this 30 years later, I smiled. But then I quit smiling. I doubt that such a thing would even be noticed today, and I'm not sure whether that is good or bad. It certainly is a reflection of our day. The principle, however, stands true: Nothing is so important that it be allowed to bring division and pain to the Body of Christ.

THE CHURCH AS
SERVANT

✦✦✦

A radio station specializing in rock music offered the local churches in its area an opportunity to present a five-minute daily program. The pastors could preach as they saw fit, but they were not to plug their own churches or give their church names and addresses. Not one pastor responded to this opportunity. Yet three of them bought time on another station so that they could promote their own churches.

I don't understand the mentality of Christians who feel that the interests of their own church must be served by everything they do—who won't serve the Lord Jesus Christ unless they can use it somehow to hook people for their own fellowship. I was talking to some people at a seminar when one of them said, "You know, I lived beside this neighbor for years. I talked to him, witnessed to him, invited him to services and told him about Jesus. When he finally began going to church, where do you suppose he went? To a Baptist church down the street!"

I said, "Praise the Lord!"

He said, "Praise the Lord? I did all the work." He felt all his work was wasted because the neighbor went to a different church.

Others have said, with mournful tones and sad faces, "I'm afraid we've lost that family to the church down the street." That's no tragedy. If my daughter moves from one bedroom in our house to another, do I consider her lost to the family? Let people get into the "room" where they belong, settle down there and grow. The name over the door doesn't matter much. What matters is that people are fed spiritually and then released back into the community to meet people's needs in Jesus' name.

East Hill is able to meet the needs of many different kinds of people. That is why they come. But we are not right for everybody. We are not the only legitimate fellowship of believers in our area. If someone chooses to attend another church, feels at home there and grows in the faith, that's great.

We are here to serve Jesus Christ, not ourselves. The church that is a force for God doesn't stand around calculating what it has to gain whenever an opportunity to serve Christ arises. It is too busy responding to the opportunities.

Serving As Christ Served

The principles of the church as servant go deeper than I have so far suggested. Jesus said, "Even the Son of Man did not come to be served, but to serve, and to give his life as a ransom for many" (Mark 10:45). Much of the church has failed to come to terms with the basic principle behind those words. Even where the words have become familiar, even where they are often cited, they are usually applied only to relationships between Christians. We miss the truth that the church is to fill a servant role in the world, as Jesus did, serving not only the brotherhood but also everyone. Paul wrote,

"As we have opportunity, let us do good to *all people,* especially to those who belong to the family of believers" (Gal. 6:10, emphasis added).

To say that the church is in the world as a servant is also to say that we are here to give, not to get. We are here to give with no strings attached and to help people because they have a need and we have resources, not because we hope to gain something.

A Place to Be Healed

One of the greatest services a church can offer a community is to provide a place for people to be brought to wholeness— to be healed physically, spiritually and emotionally. A place where people can be loved, accepted and forgiven. People are fragmented. They are torn. Life doesn't work for them because they are without Jesus. They don't need more programs and more activities. They simply need a place to be healed. The place does not have to be fancy. The physical environment need not be impressive. The people don't have to be super-spiritual. They simply need to be real, loving, accepting and forgiving.

Ingrid was a high-school girl who had blown her mind on acid (the drug of choice in the 1970s). By the time she was a junior, she claimed that she had been on 500 "trips." She was angry, rebellious and alienated. She had no Christian background or training whatsoever. She had been kicked out of every class by her teachers at Gresham High.

Ingrid first came to East Hill with a friend who made a pretense of following the Lord but soon bombed out. Ingrid would stand off in a corner, wearing a rumpled fatigue jacket, smelling like a garbage pit and emanating hostility. After she'd been hanging around like that for a while, she began coming into my office to see me. Her visits were like nothing I had ever experienced. She would simply sit on the floor and look at me for what seemed like forever, but actually was perhaps only 10 to 15 minutes. Then she would get up and walk out without having said one word.

This continued for several days straight. There would be a knock on my door, and in would come Ingrid to sit and watch me. I'd talk to her but would get no response, so I'd just continue with my work. After a while, she would get up and walk out. I sensed that something was happening in her life, but I certainly didn't understand what.

One day in the midst of one of these silent sessions, I looked over at Ingrid and saw that she was crying softly. I said, "Do you want to talk?"

"I need to receive Jesus," she said and began to pour out all the garbage of her life.

Ingrid did receive Jesus, and it was a rough road for her for a while. She came off drugs, and God began to restore her mind. She went to every one of her teachers at high school, apologized, and asked to retake her classes. Her counselor at school called me and said, "I don't know what has happened to Ingrid, but she is a completely different girl."

We had to walk Ingrid through some things. She had an alcoholic father who beat her for coming to church services. Her mother was an extreme neurotic. It was a great day when "Ink" graduated with a high grade point average. She gave me the tassel from her cap and I still have it.

Meanwhile, as God brought her to wholeness, Ink began to be burdened for other kids in trouble. She began to get acquainted with officials and chaplains in the correctional system and eventually took a job as a counselor in one of the state institutions. She shared her burden with others in the

Body, and as a result we soon had teams going each week into many of the correctional institutions in Western Oregon, with 40 to 50 of our people actively involved.

Ink is still dedicated to helping at-risk kids. Hundreds of them have felt the touch of her love and care.

Other Ways to Serve

Providing a place where hurting people can be healed will always be our primary service to the community. That does not mean that we won't serve in other ways.

When Jesus fed the 5,000, He didn't make them promise to attend His preaching services as a condition for receiving aid. He didn't extract a doctrinal statement from people before He healed them. Nor did He go to them afterward and say, "Now you owe Me one." He wanted them to believe in Him. He wanted them to be saved. He wanted them to respond. But He healed them because they were sick, and He did so knowing that some of them never would believe in Him as Savior.

I realize that when Jesus fed the 5,000, He was fulfilling prophecy and giving evidence that He was the Messiah. He was the bread from heaven who had been promised and prefigured in Moses and in the manna that fed the multitude in the wilderness. I know that when He healed the impotent man at the pool of Bethesda, He was providing a sign of His deity and that He left other sick people there untouched. His ministry was primarily a spiritual one, and His kingdom not of this world.

But does that mean He was merely using people? That when He worked a miracle, He cared nothing about individual suffering? That He only wanted to get a spiritual message across or authenticate His messianic claims? To think such things distorts not only the character of our Lord Jesus but the Word of God as well. I wonder if that might be the reason Scripture records not one but two separate incidents of Jesus feeding the multitudes. John's account of the feeding of the 5,000 clearly focuses on Jesus' fulfillment of the Mosaic prophecy (see John 6:14,30-51), but Mark's account of the feeding of the 4,000 just as clearly focuses on Jesus' compassion for the people (see Mark 8:1-3). Jesus was concerned about both His divine message and human need.

The church is in the world today as the Body of Christ to continue the work He began. As such we are to bear witness to His divine nature and mission, and we are also to show compassion to people in need. Why are we forever falling prey to the idea that we must be occupied with only one of these ministries or the other? Why can't we do both?

The church must serve the community. Jesus said, "If you love those who love you, what credit is that to you? Even 'sinners' love those who love them. And if you do good to those who are good to you, what credit is that to you? Even 'sinners' do that. And if you lend to those from whom you expect repayment, what credit is that to you? Even 'sinners' lend to 'sinners,' expecting to be repaid in full. But love your enemies, do good to them, and lend to them without expecting to get anything back" (Luke 6:32-35).

"Without expecting to get anything back." Those are key words. The *King James Version* puts it, "hoping for nothing again." We are the people of God, and that means we don't depend on this world system. We may use some of its vehicles, but we are not bound to it. We do not need its approval or support. God provides for us, and we are free to give, "hoping for nothing" in return.

Looking to Jesus As Our Source

Jesus said, "Freely you have received, freely give" (Matt. 10:8). That is the spirit in which the church must serve the world. It is true that Jesus also taught that those who give will receive abundantly, but we must not allow that to compromise the purity of our motives in giving. If we give, we will get, but we don't give in order to get—not if we obey Jesus. No, we give in order to give.

This idea of non-reciprocal living is counter to our culture. We are taught not only to get something in return but a bonus besides. We not only expect more than we get but also feel we are owed for things we have never done. Our rights, our share. We must be paid whether we work or not. We sue for more than our pain and more than our time. I am not here to correct society, but when these attitudes are allowed within the church, and especially with pastors and church leaders, it is disastrous.

One of the places this shows up in the church community is in the attitude of young pastoral candidates or those preparing for a position in the church organization. All too often when I was interviewing a candidate, I would look for a sense of calling but find a sense of career. "What's the pay? What's the chance of advancement? What are the long-term benefits?" It is certainly biblical and proper for a congregation to care for its pastors and staff. "The laborer is worthy of his hire," the *King James Version* states clearly (Luke 10:7). The apostle Paul further declared that those who teach should get "double honor" (1 Tim. 5:17). Whether or not that means twice the salary is debatable, but it certainly makes the principle of caring clear.

On the other hand, Jesus called His disciples to leave everything and expect nothing (see Matt. 16:24). That is the difference between career and calling. Does that mean we have to disregard the needs of our family? Certainly not. It means, rather, that we need to look to Jesus as our source. He has called us to a unique place of influence in His church.

God will care for and provide for those He calls. Sometimes He provides a salary. Sometimes He provides a job to supplement our ministry, as when Paul supported his ministry in Corinth with tent-making (see Acts 18:1-3). Sometimes He provides individuals who will support us with their means, as when Jesus was supported by certain "wealthy women" (see Luke 8:3). He sent ravens and fed the prophet Elijah (see 1 Kings 17:4). He sent manna and fed the children of Israel when they were following Him through the wilderness (see Exod. 16:4). I don't know what method God will use in your situation, but be sure of this: He will take care of you. The primary issue for you is His calling. He will provide for those He calls.

Ultimately, we are in His employ, not in the employ of our church or denomination. That means we must live the lifestyle that His provision dictates. We should not become caught in the upward spiral of income demand. Ours is a simple life. We want to make it as comfortable as possible, but just as economics must not determine the ministry of the church fellowship, economics must not determine our ministry. The disciples were not poverty stricken. They did not achieve sainthood through poverty. Their needs were met, and there often was something left over. That was Jesus' guarantee to them, and it is His guarantee to us.

Barbara and I have very little in terms of investments or holdings. We have budgeted our income and lived as frugally and simply as we can with what Jesus has given us. Yet as we followed Him, He took us literally around the world in ministry. He has seen to it that our children were given the opportunity of college educations. He has given us fine homes to live in and good cars to drive. He has blessed us with food and clothing. He even provided an overflow for this stage of our ministry. We have a home just the right size for the two of us on an island 20 minutes by ferry ride from Seattle. It is the island we used to come to when we were dating during our university days. We fell in love with each other and with "our" island. Now He has brought us back after nearly 50 years to work and continue our calling—and our love.

Pastoring is a call to God and God alone. It must never regress to a career. We must recapture the sense of calling in Christian ministry. When we do, this generation will take up the challenge and respond to His call.

The Church as a Force and the Education of Our Children

There is great concern among Christians these days about the quality of education and the moral climate in our public schools. And rightly so. Private Christian schools have been promoted as a solution to the problem, and they may be one alternative. However, that solution does nothing to help the public school system. To the contrary, removing the Christians tends to abandon the public school system to its doom.

We were concerned about this problem as well at East Hill, so we began to look into the problem. As we began to investigate, we discovered that the average American family with three children is involved in elementary and secondary education over a period of some 20 years. This represents the span of time from the day the oldest child enters school until the youngest child graduates. That gives families time for in-depth involvement in the educational process. In addition, in any public school system, parents can function on curriculum committees, school boards, advisory committees and parent-teacher organizations. Actually, most public schools are crying for parental involvement but getting very little.

We discovered that few of the people at our church knew both names of their child's teacher. Even fewer knew the principal's name. We couldn't find anyone who knew the superintendent's name. Few knew anything about the school board, and no one had ever served on one. Do you get the picture? Here we were crying about the public school system but behaving irresponsibly ourselves and doing nothing to improve the situation.

So we decided to take a first step and simply get the parents, the children and the school officials together. When we did, we learned several interesting things: (1) the school officials wanted to talk with the parents but hadn't found adequate ways to do so, (2) the parents wanted to talk with the school people but were afraid or didn't know how to do so, and (3) the children wanted their parents to be involved in their education and to know their teachers. The children felt totally segmented. They had a home life and a school life, and the two never met.

Our first parent-school workshop aroused so much interest that the state sent a delegation to observe whether what they had heard about was actually happening. They indicated that no church had taken on such a project before, and they were amazed. Christian teachers started coming out of the woodwork. In fact, we discovered a whole battery of Christians strategically placed throughout the school system.

We figured that with Christian parents involved and Christians working throughout the system, why abandon the whole thing to the devil? It's not that now we want to participate in the school system in a manipulative sense. We don't want to take over anything. We want to serve the community by helping to make the public school more nearly what it ought to be.

A number of these workshops were conducted at our church. We brought the parents, children and teachers together on age-graded levels. This gave them the opportunity to get to know and understand one another better. Parents learned how the system works so they could be directly involved if the Lord led them that way.

We said to teachers and administrators, "We are Christian people. We want to know how we can, with intelligence and understanding, provide the kind of input we feel necessary in the formation of the educational program. We are a part of the community, and we want to be a responsible part." Through such interaction, we helped to prepare cool, clear-eyed Christians who, when a moral issue comes up, do not grab their Bibles and start clubbing people but intelligently respond, "As a parent, this is my view . . . I have a right to this view, and you must take it into account because I am representative of a part of the community."

Such a voice is all too seldom heard. Often we are so self-righteous in our reactions that we do not serve the cause of true righteousness well.

In the past 30 years, we have seen the public school scene change dramatically. Violence is more prevalent at schools, and administrators are often less open to parental influence and are resistant to Christians. However, the principle still stands. Where we can bring healthy influence, we must. At the same time, we must not sacrifice our young people on the altar of destructive and unresponsive systems. Christian schools, charter schools, home schooling and other alternatives are available. As important as our influence in our educational community may be, our first priority is to provide a safe and quality education for our children that strengthens their Christian faith and enables them to be godly men and women to their generation. When we are no longer able to exert pressure from the inside, we are justified in designing new educational vehicles that will serve our children well and hopefully stress to the public systems from the outside the need for necessary change.

Better Homes and Gardens

A house in Portland's west hills burned down, and the man who lived there lost everything. He thought he was insured, but through some sort of slip up he was not, and he was wiped out financially.

The members of a nearby church, several of whom were carpenters and contractors, pitched in, took up offerings, supplied labor and totally rebuilt his house, without a penny coming out of his pocket. They did it simply because they felt the Lord wanted them to do it. The man was not even a member of their church.

Utterly overwhelmed by such a show of kindness, the man was solidly converted to Christ. The people who helped him had not done so because they planned to convert him in that way. They had helped him because he had a need and they had the capability to meet that need. The impact on the neighborhood was profound. People still drive by to see the "house the Christians rebuilt."

Some of the men in our church helped a woman in a somewhat similar situation. She contracted to have some remodeling done on her home. The contractor took her money but did not finish the job, leaving one whole side of her house open to the weather. The woman was contemplating going to court to sue the contractor.

Our men said, "You are going to get pretty cold if you wait on a court action to settle this. On the other hand, if you get your house fixed, you will no longer need to go to court. So let's do it that way. We'll do the job, and you can forget the lawsuit."

They didn't just shelter the woman from the weather, either. They finished that house beautifully. The result was that not only was the grateful woman rescued from her predicament but also the contractor was left scratching his head, trying to figure out just what kind of people these Christians were.

The Bible says that the believer is to "work, doing something useful with his own hands, that he may have something to share with those in need" (Eph. 4:28). Don't miss that word "share" in this verse. We hear a lot of teaching about prosperity, and some of it gives the impression that if we are not driving a Lexus or a BMW, something must be wrong with our faith. I believe that God prospers His people, but the purpose is not to make us extravagant but to make us capable of ministry.

I once traveled to the highlands of New Guinea, where people live in abject poverty. One day, my host took me into the countryside and said, "Pick out the Christians' gardens." I looked, and sure enough, the gardens of the believers were producing better than those of the non-believers. "We pray over our gardens," my host explained. "We want to grow enough food to share with our neighbors who cannot pray God's blessing on their gardens as we do."

I learned something about prosperity that day from some of the world's poorest people. I saw clearly how false it is to feel superior to others simply because one has more of this world's goods. What I am doing with my resources says infinitely more about my spiritual condition than does the fact that I have them.

A Child Will Live

I told earlier of how the Lord dealt with me about my attitude toward the children of our congregation. That was a good beginning. But what about the children in our nation and in other nations who don't have anyone to love them?

As that question burned in our hearts, Barbara and I were led to adopt an orphaned boy from India to be our fourth child and live in our home. Opening our home and our hearts in that way encouraged many other people in the congregation to do the same. I wasn't evangelistic about it. I didn't preach to the people that they should do this. I do not, in fact, believe that every family financially able to do so should adopt a child. Our doing so was a very personal thing for us, a responding in compassion to the needs of one suffering child.

As God led other members of our congregation to reach out to children in need, we saw them come into our church family in increasing numbers. Today, I would guess that there are several hundred adopted children in our congregation. Some people have adopted whole families of children. One family has 13 adopted children, all of them in the "hard to place" category because of physical defects.

One of these children, also from India, was abandoned by his mother in a garbage can when he was five. She apparently counted on him to cry loud enough for someone to rescue him. He was found and taken to an orphanage, but not until he had been in there so long that he was at the point of death. His sister, whom his mother had placed in the same garbage can, was dead.

I have been asked, "What right do you have to arbitrarily select one child, out of the masses who are just as needy, and give that child all the benefits of your home while you do nothing for the others?" I can't really answer that question, except to admit the injustice of it and to point out our need to live redemptively in an unjust world. I know that our taking one child will not mean much to the ones who are left in their suffering. But it is going to mean an awful lot to that one little boy.

I can't bring about justice in this world. I have neither the resources nor the wisdom necessary to do so. I could put myself under great condemnation because I eat well while children are starving. But what good would that do? Even if I reduced my family to a bare subsistence level, the world's poverty problem would remain virtually untouched. However, just because I cannot live justly in the world does not mean that I should do nothing—that I should ignore human need and indulge all my resources on myself. No, I am to live redemptively. I can touch this one here and that one there and make all the difference in the world to that person.

That is what Jesus did when He was here among us in the flesh. He didn't bring in the Kingdom in the sense of banishing all hunger, sickness and injustice. That glorious condition is yet to come. What He did do was touch an impotent man here and feed a hungry crowd there—and forgive the outcast sinner in yet another place. He lived redemptively.

The choice to live redemptively has a domino effect. That little two-year-old boy is now a grown man. He is a doctor of neuropsychology and has a practice near Washington, D.C. He and his wife recently had an opportunity to return to India. He was accompanied by his brother and his brother's wife. He found the church where his mother had left him shortly after his birth. He saw where he had spent his first months of life and the orphanage that had cared for him until we found him two years later.

What a joyous and incredible story our two sons and their wives shared with us when they returned home with a video of the adventure. We all cried together as we saw Sundar embracing and thanking the people who had cared for him. Some of them were elderly and were being cared for themselves at the same orphanage.

The four of them brought home a few ideas as well. For example, could we together buy a walk-in freezer and refrigerator for the orphanage? During the four days they spent as guests at the orphanage, they discovered that more than 500 people were being fed three meals a day. When they toured the kitchen, they found that plenty of food was being brought in by a grateful community but that the orphanage only had a small house refrigerator to keep it in. Much of the food being brought in had to be refused, because it would spoil in that hot tropical climate.

Our son, Jamie, discovered that there was plenty of room and electricity for the refrigerator they would need. Our family bought into the idea, and one month later the orphanage received a gift from Sundar covering the purchase and installation of the restaurant-sized walk-in refrigerator. We will continue to look for ways to help the godly people who are giving their lives to these needy children.

I was still a kid in college when I first encountered real poverty. It wasn't in a foreign land, but right here in our own country on a Navajo reservation in the Southwest. On the particular reservation I visited, 75 percent of the children either had tuberculosis or would contract it by the age of 15. Many of them would die before they reached age 20. Few would ever get off the reservation.

I remember going into that situation and seeing kids and chickens everywhere—and dogs. The kids were dirty and hungry, and I just wanted to put my arms around every one of them.

What do you do in a situation like that?

I took one little girl on my lap and hugged her. I could not embrace all of them, so I reached out to one. I showed compassion where I could not bring justice and complete deliverance.

That is where we are in the world today. We face tremendous needs. We cannot rectify all the wrongs, lift all the burdens, heal all the sick or defend all the oppressed. But we can stop and bind up the wounds of one we encounter along the way instead of passing by on the other side. Yes, and we can go out of our way as we are led by the Holy Spirit to do so in order to give a redemptive touch to someone.

THOUGHTS FOR LEADING THE CHURCH AS A FORCE

━━━━━━━━━ ❖❖❖ ━━━━━━━━━

I recently attended a church that seemed to pride itself in practicing the church-as-a-force model. "Love, Acceptance and Forgiveness" was prominently displayed in banners and included in their mission statement on the front of their bulletin. The slogans on their signs and in their literature were ministry-in-the-marketplace language. I was encouraged.

Then the service started. The worship music was contemporary and performed by talented musicians, but no one seemed to know the songs. The arrangements were masterful but so complicated that even the PowerPoint with the lyrics wasn't much help. There was an amazing disconnect between those who were leading and the worshipers. We ended up watching good musicians sing and play good songs, but we did very little worship.

One of the pastors prayed a lengthy prayer for the world, the community and the congregation, and almost equal time was given for the offering and the announcements. The list of activities presented was a grand study in media graphics. I couldn't help but think of the staff, equipment and hours it must have taken for such a production. After hearing and seeing everything going on, I was exhausted. There were groups for every conceivable configuration or taste. There were Bible classes, Bible studies, membership classes and new convert classes. There were men's meetings, women's meetings, children's meetings, youth meetings, newly married couples' meetings, board meetings—it was overwhelming. Then I looked at the bulletin and saw that it was filled with information about other special programs that hadn't made the service video cut.

The sermon was exactly 20 minutes in length (the shortest event of the morning). It included a relevant clip from a current movie, and the points were beautifully presented in video graphics. At the end of the message, the pastor informed us where we could go for prayer and have trained experts pray for us. We were then hurried out, because the service had run a little long and people were waiting for the next one to start.

Everything was done well, but I had not worshiped, had not experienced true fellowship and had not been equipped to be Jesus in my world. In fact, if I took the church schedule seriously, I would have had no time for my family let alone opportunities to cultivate meaningful relationships outside the church.

There was a huge conflict between the semantics, the public image and the structure of this church. The program expectations actually blocked the people from getting into the unbelieving community, let alone being Jesus there. Their world was reduced to the church family, which exhausted both their gifts and their time.

This is not a tirade against organization or a plea for sloppiness. Excellence and planning in what we do is important.

Well-conceived and illustrated sermons are essential. However, there must be a direct connection between who we say we are and who we are actually becoming. The things we do as a church together must not block our ability to minister individually. Church community is vital, but it must always be vehicular to our ministry in the non-believing community.

In this chapter, I want to share a few things that I have learned that will help bring this congruence. I'll start by describing two sure-fire murderers of the church as a force: micromanaging and unfocused methods of delivery.

Micromanaging

One of the great enemies to effectively leading a ministering church is the leadership style called micromanagement. It is a killer at every level. Micromanaging sends the message, "I don't trust you." It stifles initiative and blocks creativity. It has been colorfully described as a bowel obstruction in any organization. Its symptoms are a proliferation of policies, paperwork and meetings. It demands top-down structures of hierarchy: the pastor, the executive council, the directors of everything, the staff pastors, the volunteer staff and finally, if ever, the congregation.

Each of these levels is simply a means by which the pastor enacts his or her agenda and insures it is being done the way he or she wants. Everything is supposed to trickle down the ladder from the pastor's office. Anything that might start somewhere else must climb the ladder to his or her office to be ratified and reworked to his or her liking.

Although huge blocks of time may be given to brainstorming and the framing of various mission statements and goals, these exercises are only designed to give the congregants a sense of ownership while avoiding having them do any conclusive decision-making. The results of these workshops are typically tabulated by the pastor and distributed down the line along with notes on how the church is going to accomplish those goals and all the relevant expectations, paperwork and evaluative schedules that will be needed to make sure the church will be doing it right.

In smaller churches that do not have professional staff, the pastor will conduct numerous meetings with volunteer groups. The purpose of these meetings will be to air the pastor's ideas and give assignments to each person—who will then be instructed as to how those assignments are to be carried out. Then, of course, there is the usual wrestling with the church calendar, which will be finally resolved by the pastor.

Micromanaging obliterates the vision, creativity and initiative of the staff of the church, and after a short time, the strong leaders will simply not put up with it. Soon, the only people left will be those who *need* to be micromanaged—those who need to have a strict job description and be given strict rules, lunch times and office hours. The pastor may have them punch the time clock or sign in under the guise of being available, but this will only be a device for making sure that they are where they are supposed to be when they are supposed to be there. They will be held to strict policies and procedures, which will be tracked by ingenious forms that cover every area of their job description.

Without the freedom to initiate and be creative, people shrivel and die. Staff death, whether volunteer or paid, is easy to recognize:

- They come late and leave early
- They have no enthusiasm or joy in their work
- They are hypersensitive to correction or criticism

- They work hard but accomplish little
- They have a spiritual dullness
- They have low morale
- They complain frequently
- They compete with each other

Remember, if you micromanage your staff and congregation, you will never grow beyond the boundaries of your own weakness. Your leadership will not produce ministering people but rather an inward-focused group that will resemble the preceding list of the dead. You and your staff will become exhausted and burn out or drop out.

It takes time and a special kind of communication to be an effective leader. I always try to communicate a picture to those with whom I am working. I want them to see what a ministering church looks like, feels like and acts like. I want them to see who they are as they worship, converse, pray and who they are as they go about their day at home, at work or elsewhere. I want them to tell me how worship fits into this, and then we will set the boundaries of their responsibility and authority. This takes time, and I invest this time on the front end of the relationship.

I find that this area of boundary definition is often neglected in churches. So I don't give the people I work with a job description but rather an area of responsibility and broad boundaries in which they can work. I then tell them that they can take it from there. It is up to them to develop their own job description to get it done. I won't go there.

My son and his wife are currently in Swaziland with the Peace Corps. Before they could go on this assignment, they had to endure nearly two years of questionnaires, interviews and paperwork. The purpose of all this was not only for the

Corps to get a clear picture of the Jamies (both are named Jamie) but also for the Jamies to get a clear understanding of what the Peace Corps was and what a volunteer looked like, lived like, dressed like and acted like. They are now representatives of the United States of America, but they will also live with the Swazis and be one of them.

Their assignment is to develop a project that will help educate the Swazis about HIV/AIDS and bring significant change to the culture. They will care for AIDS victims during that time as well, but they must put something in place that will continue to bring growing health to this ravaged nation after they leave. Within those parameters they are completely free to develop and create whatever they want to accomplish this task, and they can draw on the Corps as a resource to do this.

This is a management model rather than a directive model. A directive model gives specific directions and individual assignments. It deals with narrow job-descriptive lists and then evaluates how well a person does on his or list. In some settings this is a valuable approach, but the management approach is much more effective for the church as a force.

Once I understand the people I am working with and they see what we are doing together and are comfortable with the boundaries, I tell them to go to it. I really don't care how they accomplish a task—the *how* is why I asked them to do something in the first place. As long as they are moral, legal, biblical and respect the parameters we have set, they are free to work in any way they want, and I will do my best to see that they have what they need to accomplish the job.

I just want to make sure that there is a direct connection between the way they are going about their assignment and the releasing of the ministry of Jesus in the lives of the people they are leading. That direct connection must be crystal clear in everything they do at every level and in every activity. If it is not, the first assumption I make is that I didn't effectively communicate the basic picture to them or that we need to adjust the boundaries. I will try again. If it still does not happen, I will assume that the person agrees but can't do it or disagrees and won't do it. We will then find someone who can and will.

Of course, this is a bit oversimplified. Relationships are never that easy, but this is the paradigm in which I endeavor to work. This is what we are trying to do together. As a pastor, I deal with the whole Body. I leave it up to the people to make sure that the arm or hand they are working with is connected to that Body and is not a transplant from some other one.

Unfocused Methods of Delivery

We had traveled all morning over supposed roads, and then by trail. We finally arrived at a remote village in the Papua New Guinea highlands. As we came into the commune of little grass huts, we were met by a smiling, sparsely dressed and elaborately tattooed and pierced villager. We quickly learned that he was the chief. He had been hunting for birds and had his bow and some arrows with him.

During a friendly conversation through my missionary friend, I asked him about his arrows. The chief explained to me that he had several different types. His bird arrows were made with several points spread out so that they would travel in a circular pattern through the air and have a better chance at hitting a bird in flight. He then brought out his war arrows and explained that they had been made to go straight to the target and pierce it. Once they hit a target, they were almost impossible to pull out because of the barbs on them.

One important lesson I learned that day was that you must always pick the arrow that fits the hunt. Don't use a bird arrow if you are going to a war. In the same way, a pastor and congregation must pick the right "arrow" that will best accomplish the goals that they have set for the church.

Through technology and creativity, pastors and congregations can launch an arrow that will travel in a broad pattern—a bird arrow. Interestingly, because of this broad pattern, the arrow will not have much range or killing power. In fact, it is possible that the arrow will end up wounding the saints instead of killing the enemy. This is what occurs when a church becomes spread out over too many programs and ministries. The church effectiveness is dissipated, and the saints are then captured, mortally wounded and lost to all that Jesus intended them to become.

You can download programs for every conceivable idea. In fact, if you don't have a good idea, you can even download one. Your "bow," your method of delivery, might be extraordinarily effective. But what are you delivering? What are you trying to do, and how do you know if you are accomplishing your goal? And is that goal really what you are supposed to be doing anyway?

There are two questions the church as a force must answer: (1) *Are we reproducing the life of Christ in our congregation?* and (2) *Are we ministering as Jesus in our world?* Everything the church does must address these two questions. The children, teens, young adults and other groups all the way through must take on the character of Jesus and be Jesus in their classrooms and activities. Every action the church community performs must serve to shape a sharp weapon that will not stagger along or lose its power. They must work to shape a weapon that will strike directly at the enemy and accomplish Kingdom business in every workplace, mall and address.

If the way we worship doesn't serve this singular purpose, then we must change. Every time we meet, in whatever configuration it may be, we must expand our worship lifestyle, experience authentic relationships, be clear in our focus and strive to become more effective in being Jesus in our world. If this is not true, we have wasted our time and forfeited Kingdom opportunity.

Life-giving Leadership

There were two services on Saturday night and three on Sunday morning. The auditorium, which seated about 800 people, was full at every service. That attendance represented a significant percentage of all the people living in that small city. Each service lasted exactly 70 minutes, but there was no sense of rushing. The worship was absolutely compelling. Every song and every comment was an invitation for people to express their praise to God.

The church's tradition for water baptism was by full immersion, and this took place throughout the worship time. When a person went to be baptized, his or her picture, name and personal testimony appeared on the large screens on each side of the platform. Each time someone came up out of the water, the singing was punctuated by loud praise and applause. There was a great sense of joy as these people publicly declared their new-found faith in Christ.

Worship continued as the offering baskets were passed. Everyone understood that his or her giving was worship, too. They were also given time to join in small circles and pray for one another. The language the speakers used was clear and devoid of religious jargon or church phrases. It was the way people really talk.

I was the guest speaker that weekend. Amazingly, I had plenty of time to teach. I endeavored to help people see the wonder and greatness of God and understand that through the Holy Spirit, His presence and power could be theirs as they went into their places of ministry this week. All through that weekend, people came to embrace Jesus as their Savior. They were healed, encouraged and ready to be Jesus at the point of their strategic ministry location.

I am not telling this story to suggest that we should all run our public services this way. There is no particular *way* to do church as a force. However, I do want to underline several things that must be true in all our church life if we are to effectively release Jesus through the people we lead. In the church I spoke at that weekend, the services were more than just technique. There were many things in place at the very heart of the congregation and leadership that made such a valuable gathering possible. Let's examine of few of these.

Authenticity

Authenticity means that there is a direct connection at a personal level between the platform, the seats and the shopping mall. I was once given a beautiful portfolio of wonderful art. Each piece was a portrait of Christ. They were so vivid and fine that it was hard to view them without a tear. The title of the work was, "He Was One of Us." What a great description of Christ! It is also a great definition of authenticity. Effective church-as-a-force leaders must be seen by the people they are endeavoring to lead as being one of them.

It is a great mistake to confuse authenticity with full disclosure. Even Jesus refused to disclose Himself fully to everyone. Transparency does not mean that everyone has to know everything about you. (You don't even *want* to know everything about me!) What it does mean is that what others do know really is you. You are not projecting or protecting some image. It means that you don't have a hidden life that you are afraid somebody will stumble into. It means that when you have a chance encounter with somebody at the mall or in the restaurant, or if someone happens by your house unannounced, you are the same person that they saw on Sunday morning.

I was once speaking at a conference in Greece. Barbara and I were staying in a hotel directly in the center of Athens, which happened to be a place that hosted various Orthodox church events. Many priests and church officials were coming and going. As these men dressed in their robes and high hats stood conversing, people would approach them, bow down and kiss a huge ring on their finger. I watched this with great curiosity. Not once did the officials acknowledge any of these people. The holy (or not so holy) conversation continued, while the holy finger was extended, kissed and withdrawn automatically. The person remained non-existent. I couldn't help but wonder what the person's view of God was, when His representative treated him or her as invisible.

This is the radical extreme of what I am talking about. Authentic leaders convey not only what they believe or think but also their emotions. When something is funny, they laugh. When it's tragic or deeply moving, they cry. When there is evil and injustice, they are angry. They realize that they can't really know a person until they understand how he or she *feels*. They don't convey an image; they present their person. Even their preaching presents truth through their personality.

Clear Models

Authentic leaders will also illustrate how Jesus walks with us in life—what living with God looks like when we are celebrating, mourning or suffering physical anguish. They share their own journey. Now, this does not mean that every Sunday is a rehearsal of their problems and issues. It does not mean that their sermons are little autobiographical sketches. It simply means that these leaders are real people, living in a real world, endeavoring to figure out what godliness looks and lives like.

Authentic leaders' public prayer and private prayers with individuals serve as models to the congregation of how to talk to God even in the grocery store. Their public teaching is not only understandable but also translatable into life. They talk about Jesus on Sunday in ways their listeners can talk about Him on Monday. Sunday is a workshop on how to bring Jesus to their world.

This modeling is not just for the pastor but also for all leaders throughout the entire church family. This kind of *real* is the standard for all leaders, whether paid or volunteer. The leaders' relationships with one another and with the congregation must illustrate what is meant by love, acceptance and forgiveness. People must be able to meet Jesus and experience His presence in their leaders if they are to be Jesus in their world.

Natural Networks

Today, there is a great emphasis on the establishment of small groups in congregations. I understand the reason for some of this. But, like many other good ideas, we have sought to make these groups programs of the church, and they often become burdened down with complex administrative problems.

At least this illustrates that we have finally discovered the demand for meaningful relationships. Being truly Christian is not just a matter of us and Jesus; it is us, our brothers and sisters and Jesus. We are not only part of a community but also part of a communion of saints. However, the way we are going about doing these groups does seem to demand an awful lot of money, energy and work for a relatively small return in reaching and discipling people.

Have you noticed that most people have friends? Have you also noticed that most visitors to our services are there with a friend? It is also noteworthy that most sermons are discussed and questions and problems disclosed among friends before anywhere else.

In Jesus' commencement address to His disciples a few days before His death, He announced, "I no longer call you servants, because a servant does not know his master's business. Instead, I have called you friends" (John 15:15). In that brief but dramatic statement, Jesus forever elevated friendship to the highest relationship between God and humans and, therefore, between human and human as well.

However we choose to structure our church community, we must not disrupt the natural friendship networks that people have—especially their networks outside the believing community. Of course, some lifestyles and relationships are so destructive that they must be broken (this is true whether the people involved are Christians or not). But do you remember how often Jesus told those He healed or delivered to go back to their own village or town? The incredible stories of the Samaritan woman He gave a drink at the well and the demoniac He delivered in the cemetery of Gadara rippled through the entire area in which they lived, and as a result many put their faith in Jesus.

In our church, we saw firsthand how powerful natural networks could be. For example, a truck driver came to Christ, and before long a whole bunch of truck drivers were coming to be baptized. A downtown pimp got saved, and all his "girls" except one came to Christ and began to lead healthy and healed lives. The president of a local outlaw biker gang came to Christ, and Jesus transformed that entire bunch of gangsters into one of the first Christian biker clubs on the West Coast. We had a run on lawyers, politicians and then neighbors and schoolmates. The reason for all of this was because we didn't try to break up the natural friendship networks of new believers by demanding they join already existing groups with people they didn't know or may not have even liked. Entire networks came to Christ, and these rippled into the second- and third-generation networks that were represented as well.

What I am saying is that it is important for us to validate friendships. We need to teach people the value of being a godly friend. Even if their friends do not become Christians, every person deserves to experience the love of Jesus through a godly friend. Jesus said that friends will even die for one another (see John 15:13), and a few days later, He died as our friend.

As Christians in whom Jesus lives, we are the only people who can establish a true friendship with another person. Because our fulfillment comes from our relationship with Him, we do not have to parasite off our friends to get our needs met or our egos stroked. We can truly give and gratefully receive with no strings attached and no hidden agendas.

The Leader as Friend

Leaders in the church as a force cannot just teach about friendship and relationships. They must also be a friend and establish meaningful relationships themselves. The old idea that they must not have close friends in the congregation is not only ridiculous but also unbiblical. Jesus' example buries that idea in an iron casket and a deep grave. The old saying "familiarity breeds contempt" (hopefully you have never heard it) is only true if a person is contemptible.

The pastor who preaches great sermons and then slips out the back door because he or she is too shy or too tired or too whatever will only be a voice and never a person to his or her people. It was only when the voice of God became the "Living Word" and wrapped itself in a human flesh-and-blood person that we came to understand God and His love. He became one of us. That is the divine pattern, and we will not find any effective detour. Pastors certainly don't need to confine their friendships only to the congregation, but the sheep they pastor must be included in their friendship. If they are to follow, they must know the shepherd. They will not follow a stranger.

When pastors bring a validation and model of godly friendship, they will save the church money and reduce the size of their staff. What is the reason for this? Because friends take care of friends. When they are sick, their friends visit them.

In my recent battle with cancer, one of my friends was with me almost every day for what became more than a year of surgery and treatments. The few times he couldn't be with me because of chemo or radiation or some other complication, he would call me, often several times a day. Other friends took off work and traveled from other cities to be with me, to feed me, clean me up and care for me and give Barbara much needed rest.

When someone starts missing the church gatherings or gets careless in his or her Christian practices, a friend steps in and asks why. When someone's theology gets a bit goofy, a friend can invite him or her to turn around, bend over and then administer the much-needed kick in the pants along with a loving, "straighten up."

We need supportive programs and groups in the church, but we must never take over the ministry of friendship. We can't fall into the false obligation of thinking that we have to organize everyone's social life, family life and calendar. In all the organizing, we must be sure not to violate or minimize the power of natural friendship networks.

So, What Can I Do?

An older pastor described his historic congregation to me as being full of wonderful people who liked their church the way it was and weren't about to change. A middle-aged pastor told me about the congregation he had recently come to, which was fairly traditional and heavily in debt due to a new building. A young pastor told me about the congregation he was just establishing in a fast-growing metropolitan area. They all had the same question: *What should I do to help us become a church as a force?*

I must admit that of the three, I would prefer the third. Change can be painful, and institutional change, especially one with religious overtones, is much like turning an elephant in an elevator: very difficult, very slow and very messy. Institutions, by their very nature, resist change. Remember, the church is people, not structures. It is common to change structures or programs and not change the people. We then inject confusion, sponsor divisions and engender disappointment.

Let me mention a few points that might help the process, regardless of what your situation might be.

Identify a Healthy Core

It is my conviction that groups change from the center—the core—and not from the outer parameters. In other words, pressure comes from the inside out, not from the outside in. Pressure from the edge can change the shape of things, but it seldom alters the substance of the group itself. For this reason, it is important to identify a healthy core of people. They may or may not be the current visible leaders or office holders.

I identify these people by looking for "lights" and "life." When I talk about my understanding of the church as a force, I look for those eyes that light up and the people who come to life. I'm not even pushing for understanding. I'm just looking for a pulse.

These people may be in a group I'm talking to or just part of a casual conversation. When I see them, I will begin to engage in some process of ongoing conversation. I am looking for a test group—people who will join me in becoming what I am talking about. I intentionally pastor these people, though not to the exclusion of the rest of the congregation (I am the shepherd of all the sheep). Note that it doesn't take a huge number of these individuals to effect dramatic change in the church. And, if the people are truly on the same page, it doesn't take an enormous amount of time for change to occur. Once a concept is born and health begins, it feeds on itself and grows.

When our church was still young, I spoke one morning to about 50 people who were present. I talked about the church being "the body of Christ," as Paul describes it in Ephesians. After the service, two of the young men (we were all young then) came to me and said, "We'd really like to understand what that means." I replied, "So would I." So Barbara and I, those two men and their wives and one other couple decided to meet on Wednesday evenings at one of their homes and talk about it. We met faithfully for perhaps a year or more. We weren't an official anything. We didn't announce the group in the church bulletin. We didn't try to grow or reproduce ourselves. I'm not sure the rest of the congregation even knew that we met, or that they cared for that matter.

We began reading Ephesians together, endeavoring to answer the question, *What does it mean to be the Body of Christ in our community?* We actually became our own answer. Jesus taught us and changed us. He challenged us and prodded us beyond all our boundaries and biases. We would read and talk about what the Body of Christ could possibly mean. Then, after a while, the women would convene for their important talk, and we men would get out the guitars and banjo and sing every crazy song we could think of. We would lug our poor sleepy children back to their own beds sometime in the wee morning hours. This little group became the core of our congregation. They set the tone for who we would become.

Tell Stories

I have discovered that as the influence of this kind of core grows into the chemistry of the church, change begins. Stories begin to surface, and these living parables must be given a hearing. Stories define who we are and what we are about. We don't really know a person until we know his or her story.

We don't know who we are as a group of people until we hear our story and someone says, "Yes, that's us."

I am a gatherer of stories. I am a storyteller. I love stories. I listen for them. I repeat them. I try to get you to tell me yours. And then, I try to get you to tell it to the congregation. If you won't or can't, I seek permission to tell it in your name.

I am not describing what a few old-timers might call "testimonies," which are usually repetitive accounts told by repeat testifiers of things that do not require God to accomplish. Or they are statements of things that have been true for a long time—good, but old: "I was saved, sanctified, filled with the Spirit [or whatever term your theology would allow] and going to heaven." That's great. I am happy for you. We are all happy for you. We have been happy for you for the last 10 years. But the story of a life transformed, of a bondage broken and a body healed in a way that only God could have done is electrifying, especially when it happened last Tuesday.

A friend of ours was staying at our house for a few days. He had been suffering with a heart arrhythmia problem. He mentioned to me a dream that he had been having persistently. Satan came to him and told him that he was going to die. He would wake terrified and sweating. It upset him so much that he couldn't sleep. I called Barb, and we prayed in Jesus' name. That night, he slept through the night, and the dream has never returned.

This story illustrates the fact that common people like you and me can have our prayers answered. I want you to know that. I am not looking for the big stuff, nor do I look to the same storytellers every time. Rather, I look for the Jans or Johns that are just us—those individuals whose lives were beautifully invaded by the presence of Jesus. One such couple in our church stood up together, and the husband said, "We were going to get a divorce a few weeks ago. Then Tom and Nancy here introduced us to Jesus. For the first time, we really have a home now."

Another woman in our church, Lilly, was 85 years old. While I visited her one time, she went to her closet and brought out a little box. She took some papers from the box and handed me one of the poems she had written. She told me that she had written it when she received word that her son had been killed in World War II. It was a remarkable description of a mother's love for her son.

Since the next Sunday was Mother's Day, I asked Lilly if she would be willing to read the poem in all the services that weekend. She said, "Oh, no. I could never get up in front of all those people. You read it." I told her it wasn't my story and that they needed to hear her. "I just couldn't face them," she replied. "Well," I said, "what if I stood there with you and held the microphone? You could turn your back on them and read it to me." She agreed that maybe she could do that.

Lilly was shaking when she timidly came to the platform after I introduced her and told the story of the poem. I turned her around to face me, with her back to the audience. In a frail voice, she read a mother's heart to her son. Not only was there not a dry eye in the place, but also the entire congregation of more than 1,000 people jumped to their feet in a standing, prolonged ovation. Lilly looked at me and quietly asked, "Was that okay?" "They are not crying and clapping for me," I answered and gave her a hug from everyone in the congregation.

That weekend, the response was the same in every service. The church learned what we meant when *we* said, "mother."

Another man named Bill stood nervously at m.,
and told his story to the congregation. He said that he wasn'
sure what all was going on, but that the terrible anger he had
lived with for years and failed miserably to control had left
him three weeks ago during the worship time. "My wife even
noticed," he announced, which of course was the proof of
the pudding.

Just as "the Word became flesh and lived with us" so
many years ago, He must live among us again. Of course, He
is the "only begotten of the Father," which means that there
is and always will be only one of Him. I understand that and
believe that. But I also believe that He lives in us through the
Holy Spirit today and that He is therefore present in us today. The principle still holds true: what we are trying to communicate must become flesh and live among us. "Jesus is
alive" has to be more than a billboard or bumper sticker. He
has to be alive *in us!*

Those of us who talk about Jesus must live like Jesus.
Those of us who talk about power must illustrate His power.
Those of us who talk about faith must illustrate what faith
looks like in shoes, slippers and bare feet. Pastoring a core of
people can give this living incarnation of what we are trying
to say.

Build a Group of Interpreters

It was Sunday afternoon and Chuck, a man in whom I had
seen the light and life I talked about, invited two other couples to lunch with him and his wife. One of the couples was
new to the church; the other had been there awhile. They
were talking about the service, and the wife of the newer couple repeated one of my statements from that morning. She
thought it was interesting, but was not sure what I meant.

The husband of the couple who had been attending for some time immediately began to explain, "I know that's what Jerry said, but this is what he meant." He then went on to completely miss my point. Fortunately, Chuck and his wife knew exactly what I meant and brought an accurate interpretation and further explanation to my words.

As pastors' sphere of influence grows, they will need to communicate more and more through their interpreters. If they are wise, they will have their "Chucks"—their core—to accurately convey what they have said. Many leaders fail because they do not know who their interpreters are and do not develop a knowledgeable core of people who know them and understand what they mean when they talk.

If pastors are to lead the church as a force effectively, their people must see clearly and hear accurately what they are talking about. They must *be* the person they want their church to become, and they must teach the people to do the same. The person I am referring to is Jesus. We really are "the church, which is his body, the fullness of him who fills everything in every way" (Eph. 1:22-23).

Ending with a Comma

I have told various people that this book will not end with a period. I cannot end it with a period, because it is an incomplete statement. I haven't given the final word on the church as a force. I am still learning to hear what the Lord has to say about living for Him as a body of believers on this planet.

No doubt the Lord has things to teach us that I do not yet sense even dimly. Even now He is saying new things to us about learning the Christian lifestyle and about the use of our resources. So this is not the end of the story. It is, however, a place to stop, the place to write the closing "comma."

Postscript

A lot has happened since the comma ended the first writing. This book has been translated into numerous languages, and I have followed to places in Europe, Asia and the South Pacific. It has pressed its way into colleges, seminaries and business organizations.

In Okinawa, I spoke to 50 single moms who knew nothing about Christ. I then went to a nursing home and spoke to men and women, many of whom were over 90 years old. One was 108 years old. They all listened eagerly and wanted to talk with me longer than I could stay. We talked about love, acceptance and forgiveness. Not the book—they knew little if anything about that, only that I had written it. They wanted to hear about a God who loves them and accepts them and forgives them.

I spoke in a packed theater in Nagoya, Japan. When I was finished, men and women of every age crowded me on the platform. They were weeping. They patted me and squeezed my hands and arms. The fact that someone would tell them of their value and lovability—that God accepted and forgave them—brought a rare flood of emotion to these wonderful people.

Hundreds, perhaps thousands (I have not counted), have written and emailed me over the years. Some have even called from foreign countries to tell me their stories and thank me for writing this little book.

I know very little about church structure, church buildings or the lack of them. I do know that we are as fractured a culture as we were 30 years ago, and perhaps more so. I still see the tears and open hearts when I talk about love, acceptance and forgiveness.

I could never have envisioned the past 30 years, and I certainly cannot predict the next. I do not believe, however, that we will ever outgrow our thirst to be loved or our desire for acceptance or our desperate need for forgiveness from one another, and especially from God.

Whatever form it takes, it will be the ones who love who will have those to love; the ones who accept who will have those who need acceptance; and the ones who are willing to forgive who will have those who need forgiveness. They will find us, just as they found Christ. When they do, may they also discover the Father He revealed—the One who is Himself love—who opens His arms in acceptance and with joy offers them forgiveness.

STUDY GUIDE

The Plan

This study guide is designed to help you form a clear and practical understanding of the church and its ministry in the world. But the effort is not just to give you information on the subject. I want you to be a vital part of what I call "the church as a force."

If you carefully and conscientiously deal with the questions, develop the discussions and seriously think through the evaluations, you will not only become knowledgeable of the material but also proficient in its application to your life. I have tried to design the questions and interactions in such a way that they will cause you to deeply consider and understand the implications of these concepts and live them out naturally and consistently. The purpose of these questions is not merely to produce an answer but to provoke true learning.

It is through each believer that Jesus invades a fallen, hurting and hungry world. You will never be successful in getting enough unbelieving people (even though they may be interested) inside the church building to make any serious impact in the world, no matter how user friendly the services and programs may be. The reason is simple: unbelieving people don't want to go to church for the same reason you didn't when you were where they are.

That's why the Great Commission is not "get everybody in" but "go into all the world." Once people see the love, acceptance and forgiveness of Jesus in *you* and realize that the church is made of people like you, they will often desire both Jesus and the church. However, should they never make this choice, all people should have the opportunity to experience the love and presence of Jesus. This book and study guide will help define and equip you for that exciting and incredibly effective adventure. It will encourage and teach you to be *you, filled with Him, open for business.*

It is important that you read *Love, Acceptance and Forgiveness* in its entirety before attempting to work through this study guide. Although the guide is based on the consecutive chapters of the book, an overall understanding of the viewpoint presented is essential to maximizing your personal study.

CHAPTER 1

A Place Where People Are Made Whole

1. On page 12, I make the following statement about the importance of love, acceptance and forgiveness:

   Love, acceptance, forgiveness—those three things are absolutely essential to consistently bring people to maturity and wholeness. If the church—the living presence of Christ in His people—is to be the force for God in the world that it should be, it must learn to love people, accept them and forgive them.

   Why are these qualities absolutely essential?

   What is the relationship between love, acceptance and forgiveness and being a force for God in the world?

2. Unless love, acceptance and forgiveness are guaranteed, a person will not risk the honesty and openness required for true wholeness. What is it about these three that establishes this degree of safety?

3. *Agape* love is a volitional commitment we make to another that motivates us to act on his or her behalf (see page 14). What does *agape* love mean to you?

    How do your emotions fit in with this type of love?

    How does commitment pertain to this kind of love?

    In your experience, how does this idea compare with usual concepts of love, both inside and outside the church?

4. On pages 14-15, I state the following about the commitment required in love:

    I want you to know that I'm committed to you. You'll never knowingly suffer at my hands. I'll never say or do anything, knowingly, to hurt you. I'll always in every circumstance seek to help you and support you. If you're down and I can lift you up, I'll do that. Anything I have that you need, I'll share with you; and if need be, I'll give it to you. No matter what I find out about you and no matter what happens in the future, either good or bad, my commitment to you will never change. And there's nothing you can do about it. You don't have to respond. I love you, and that's what it means.

What strikes you the most about this statement?

Are there people in your life now with whom you have this kind of relationship? Name some of them.

Are you aware of anyone who views you this way in his or her life?

What kind of problems and challenges does this type of commitment raise?

What are your feelings and thoughts when you think of an environment in which this attitude prevails?

5. A working definition of *agape* love is "choosing to act for another person's highest good." Would the other person's "highest good" necessarily be what he or she would describe as "loving"? Why or why not?

What are the dangers that this idea of love could become an enabling of another person's destructive behavior?

What are some specific ways you can tell when this delicate line is crossed?

In what ways is love essentially a choice?

6. On page 21, I state, "Because we are accepted in the Beloved, we must be accepting of the beloved." What are some of the implications of this statement?

Have you noticed a connection between knowing God has accepted you and your ability to accept another? Give an example from your own experience.

7. A working definition of acceptance is "releasing another from the need to qualify or perform for another's love and attention." Can you recall a situation in which you felt rejected by someone and knew that you would never be accepted by this person in that situation? Describe that event.

    How did this experience make you feel? Describe the emotions you felt.

    Can you describe a time when you were unconditionally accepted even before the person really knew you?

    How did this experience make you feel? Describe the emotions you felt.

8. Review the discussion of forgiveness beginning on page 23. Catherine Marshall suggests that forgiveness is releasing another person from our own personal judgment. Is it possible to forgive a person without implying that what they have done is okay or, at least, not so bad? Give some examples.

9. A working definition of forgiveness is "choosing not to punish a person for something that he or she did to you." What are some specific ways you tend to punish people for hurting, mistreating or disappointing you?

    In your experience, what are some of the results of punitive relationships between:

    · Husbands and wives?
    · Parents and children?
    · Friends?

10. What does the statement "forgiveness is a lifestyle, not just an event" mean to you?

11. "Love is not license; acceptance is not agreement; forgiveness is not compromise." Using each of these statements as a lens, apply the material you have read in this chapter to the following relationships in your life. Be as specific as possible, and ask the Holy Spirit to help you see these individual people through Jesus' eyes. How does this concept of love, acceptance and forgiveness change your view of:

- Your spouse?
- Your children? (Give examples with each child.)
- Your immediate family—your parents, uncles, aunts, nephews, nieces, cousins?
- Your friends? (Give examples of some friends and describe each through these three lenses.)
- Your church family?
- Your fellow workers? (Name some of your coworkers who especially bother you the most and apply these lenses to your viewpoint.)
- The stranger crossing your path?
- The homeless person carrying a sign at the intersection?
- The angry road-raging driver on the freeway?
- The grocery clerk at the local shopping center?
- The waitress/waiter at a restaurant you frequent?
- The teenage skateboarder with green hair, tattoos and piercings?
- Your own life?

12. Write out a prayer asking God to help you apply the principles you have learned in this chapter to each of your relationships.

CHAPTER 2

The Need for a Guiding Philosophy

In this chapter, I endeavor to lay the groundwork for the development of a clear guiding philosophy of ministry and church life. I discuss the need for such a philosophy and the danger that results from not having one. Now, by a "guiding philosophy," I do not mean some vague or complex theory. It is rather the need for a defined and clear foundation that can be used to evaluate everything we do as well as answer effectively the "why" questions.

1. What three things listed on page 27 result when the leadership of a church does not have well-defined guiding philosophy? Give an example of each from your own personal experience.

2. As I mention on page 28, one basic premise in my own philosophy of the church is that *the people themselves are the ministers*. This is the primary theme of this book. What are some of your thoughts about this idea?

   What are the implications of applying this principle to the concept of church life?

3. On page 28, I state that "it is not the pastor's job to meet everybody's need. It is the pastor's job to see that

everybody's need is met." How does this idea fit in with your own beliefs and experience?

4. Review the discussion of church fads on pages 29-33. Which of these fads do you observe in church life today?

    Why do you think these are fads and not legitimate trends?

5. On page 32, I suggest that the church "should not be as concerned about being 'relevant' as being prophetic." We in the church need to be a prophetic presence in the world and be speaking what God is speaking to the world. What are three major issues you see facing our culture right now that need the church's prophetic insight?

    If Jesus were living in our country right now, how would He deal with each of these issues?

6. On page 33, I note that "the dynamic for church growth is Spirit-filled people meeting other people's needs in Jesus' name wherever they are." Why would this dynamic effect church growth?

    What would happen if this principle were actually applied? (Let your imagination run with this one!)

    How does this statement effect your own particular Christian experience?

7. What is the distinction between our planting churches and Jesus planting people?

8. Review the discussion on pages 33-36 about worship traditions in the church. What is the distinction between "tradition" and "traditionalism"?

   In your opinion, what are the dangers of traditionalism in church life?

   What are some current examples of traditionalism?

9. What is your personal understanding and experience of corporate worship? Of the sermon? Of public prayer?

10. On page 35, I write, "We should not see valid forms of ministry as vehicles to something else." What do you understand this statement to mean?

11. In this chapter, we have looked at the pastor and church life in general. Now take some time to apply these ideas to your own life. As an individual Christian, what is your personal philosophy of ministry?

    What specific ideas in this chapter challenged your thinking the most?

CHAPTER 3

The Church as a Force

In this chapter, which represents the heart of the book, I paint a picture of the church as a ministering force in the world. This is not just a change in semantics but also a change in our entire perception of the church and its purpose. This viewpoint does away with the idea that the church is a place where religious activities take place and that the pastor is primarily an activities director. With the church-as-a-force model, we begin to see the implications of the church as a people who are individually and collectively living out the life and purposes of Christ in their world.

The Church as a Field

1. How would you define the "church as a field"?

2. What is the emphasis of the church as a field?

3. What are its goals?

4. What does it understand its ministry to be?

5. How is this ministry accomplished?

6. There are several dangers listed on pages 45-48 that this idea of church faces. Can you think of others?

7. What is the ultimate outcome for a church that adopts this model?

The Church as a Force

1. How would you define the "church as a force"?

2. What differences take place when you define the church personally rather than institutionally?

3. What does the church as a force emphasize?

4.   On page 49, I make the following statement about the church as a force:

> The church as a force emphases are worship, training and fellowship, because these are the things that produce Spirit-filled people who can meet others' needs in Jesus' name.

Why does worship produce Spirit-filled ministering people?

Why does training produce Spirit-filled ministering people?

Why does fellowship produce Spirit-filled ministering people?

5.   What are the three goals for the church as a force?

What is your definition of "wholeness"?

What do you consider to be essential in order for believers to be released into the world to minister?

6.   On page 51, I state that Ephesians 4:12 is "foundational to the concept of the church as a force." What is your understanding of the phrase "prepare God's people for works of service"?

How would you define "ministry"?

Who is supposed to give this preparation according to Ephesians 4:12?

How does this preparation take place?

What would be the potential results if every church focused on equipping and releasing its members into ministry?

What are the greatest inhibitors to this potential being realized?

7. On page 51, I state, "The automatic result of great healing is great outreach." A friend of mine says that "ministry flows from healing, and great ministry flows from great healing." What experiences of healing in your life would you say have the potential of bringing healing to others?

How does this principle effect the way you respond to the pain or trauma in your own life?

8. On page 58, I note that "[many Christians] know what they are saved *from* and what they are saved *to*, but not what they are saved *for*." What do you understand this statement to mean?

9. The underlying theme for the discussion of the ministry of the church as a force on pages 51-55 is that we are where we are and who we are *on purpose*. We are called to be "open for business" in our world. What do you understand the phrase "open for business" to mean?

How would you evaluate your present situation at work and in your neighborhood in terms of this principle?

What unique people, situations and opportunities exist in those places?

10. Write out a prayer asking Jesus to show you what being "open for business" means right now at your address. Leave the back of that prayer sheet blank and make notes as God shows the answer to you.

CHAPTER 4

People Equipped to Serve

If we are to be part of the church as a force, we must understand who we are in terms of our standing and identity in Christ. We must also understand what we have in terms of being adequately equipped to accomplish our destiny. In this chapter, we looked at the remarkable plan Jesus has invoked to continue His presence and power in the arena of everyday life—*our everyday life.*

1. Review the discussion on pages 61-67 on how the gifts of the Spirit are God's means of getting to people in the marketplace and meeting their needs through us. Give some examples of this "marketplace" giftedness in the life of Jesus.

   Sometimes, these gifts can be expressed so naturally through us that we may not be aware what is taking place. Have you ever experienced anything like this? If so, describe the event.

What are some ways you could see this taking place in your life on a more consistent basis?

2. On page 66, I state, "The leadership of the church has sinned against the Body of Christ by communicating to God's people that they are not fit to serve Him." What does this statement mean to you? Explain your answer.

3. Review the discussion in this chapter on the two equipping forces in the life of the believer. What are those two equipping forces?

   Which would you say is the more important of the two?

   Do you think the above is a proper question? Why or why not?

   On what basis would you evaluate these equipping forces as to their importance?

4. What percentage of the day would you say that you are aware of the presence of the Holy Spirit in your everyday affairs?

5. What are three specific things you can do today to help you be more aware of the presence and gifts of the Holy Spirit in your everyday life?

6. Evaluate your exposure to the Word of God. What are three specific ways you can allow the Word to more effectively equip you for ministry?

CHAPTER 5

Released to Minister

All the equipping and training in the world will be of little effect if people are not trusted and released to minister. To be released doesn't mean to be authorized by a religious organization or some official ministry. That can be valuable in certain instances, but all believers have been authorized, filled with and anointed by the Holy Spirit to be the effective presence of Jesus in their world. The issues are trust and permission. This chapter deals with these two points and addresses their importance in giving people confidence to simply be who they are, filled with Him, open for business in a natural and authentic way.

1. There are four principles that are essential to releasing people into ministry:

    · Trust in the innate power of the gospel
    · Trust the life of Christ in the believer
    · Remember whose church it is
    · Embrace the "Immanuel Principle"

    What is your understanding of each of these principles?

2. What would you say is the difference between religion and Christianity?

    What are the implications of God seeking or reaching out for people as opposed to the idea of people seeking and reaching out for God?

How do you understand yourself to be one of the ways that God uses to seek and reach people?

What is the implication of this in your life? Give some examples of how this has actually taken place in your own situation.

3. On page 76, I state that "people don't need a warden to guard them; they need a shepherd to guide them." How does this attitude change a leader's approach and relationship with this congregation?

   How does this attitude change the chemistry and "feel" of a group of people?

4. Was there ever a time when you did not feel "authorized" to minister? Describe the circumstances and why you felt this way.

   What would have made you feel released to minister?

5. What is your response to the idea that we are to love people in Jesus' name rather than recruit them for the church or "convert" them to Christianity?

6. In your own life, how are you being the presence of Jesus in your world?

   How are the struggles and victories you have experienced or are experiencing equipping you to minister?

   Into what segment of the culture does your work arena lead?

What are you doing to maximize this opportunity?

Do you need a better strategy?

How would you evaluate your social and neighborhood networks from the same perspective?

CHAPTER 6

The Families of the Force

In this chapter, I discuss the profound implications of love, acceptance and forgiveness in the home and family. These qualities bring health wherever they are lived out—in our church, in our marriage and in our homes.

1. What is the source of God's love (*agape*) (see page 89)?

    What is the working definition of *agape* love?

    Agape love is always connected with the idea of giving. What are the implications of this in a family?

    How does the dynamic of a family or marriage change when the focus is on giving rather than receiving?

    How would you rate your own attitude in this regard?

    Would the other members of your family agree with you? Why or why not?

2. On page 90, I note, "One of the greatest love gifts you can give your partner in marriage is total, unqualified *acceptance*." What is the working definition of acceptance?

   What are several specific ways that you express acceptance to your family?

   How do the members of your family respond when you express this type of acceptance?

   Do you ever express non-acceptance? If so, in what ways?

   How do the members of your family respond to this?

   How do you convey acceptance to your spouse or children when there is disagreement or a need for parental discipline?

3. On page 92, I state that "along with love and acceptance, forgiveness is one of the most healing elements in a home or church." What is the working definition of forgiveness?

   What does it mean that forgiveness must not just be an event but a lifestyle?

4. Whatever you plant grows. "If you want a good home, build an environment that grows good homes" (page 96). What is your home environment like? List both positive and negative characteristics.

   What seeds have you sown to produce this environment?

What changes would you like to see in your home environment?

What seeds can you plant to produce those changes?

5. Ultimately, the family is responsible for the spiritual growth of its children. What specific things are you doing in your family to nurture this spiritual growth in your children?

What role does the church family have in this effort?

What about children from unbelieving families?

CHAPTER 7

Dealing with Difficulties

In this chapter, I discuss a few of the difficulties that can arise when we attempt to apply the principles of love, acceptance and forgiveness in the life of the church. The central statement is on page 103: "Welcoming difficulties in the life of the church isn't easy. Yet every difficulty that arises presents an opportunity for growth, either for individual members or for the corporate body. The church's difficulties are either problems with people (the resolution of which should lead to personal growth) or problems with practice (the resolution of which should lead to corporate growth)."

1. Four people-related difficulties that often arise in a fellowship include "criticism," "sensitivity," "divisiveness" and "traditionalism." Can you think of any others?

2.   Why is criticism so damaging (see pages 103-105)?

Can you recall a recent time when you were criticized? Describe the situation.

Is there such a thing as "constructive criticism"? If so, how would you describe it?

Have you ever been "constructively criticized"? If so, how did it make you feel?

3.   What is the distinction between being sensitive to others and sensitivity, as I am using it in this chapter (see pages 105-107)?

Why is being quick to take offense damaging to close and safe relationships?

4.   What usually motivates divisiveness in a group (see pages 107-109)?

Have you ever been involved in a divisive situation? If so, what were the effects on the group?

What are some healthy ways to handle differences?

5.   On page 116, I ask, "How can a big church stay person-centered?" What is the answer to this question?

What is meant by "person centeredness"?

What are some examples of a person-centered church?

6. I close this chapter with the statement, "If we have a solid philosophical base in the principles of the church as a force, we can deal with difficulties and come out stronger in the process" (page 119). What does this statement mean to you?

Can you give some illustrations of this from your own experience?

Will this principle also work at home? At work? Explain and illustrate.

CHAPTER 8

The Church as Servant

This chapter sums up the spirit and heart of the book. The statement on pages 121-122 states it succinctly:

> We miss the truth that the church is to fill a servant role in the world, as Jesus did, serving not only the brotherhood but also everyone. . . . To say that the church is in the world as a servant is also to say that we are here to give, not to get. We are here to give with no strings attached and help people because they have a need and we have resources, not because we hope to gain something.

1. Why is it impossible for the church as a field to be a true-servant presence in the culture?

2. To serve means simply to become available to another's need. What are several ways you have devised to do this personally?

   In your marriage, home and family?

   At your work or place of business?

   To your neighbors?

3. Are there ways you can adjust your thinking to more consistently maintain a servant lifestyle?

4. Do you consider your church to be a place of healing? What attitudes would need to be adopted to make that happen?

   In addition to being a place of healing, what are other ways the church can serve the community?

5. On page 127, I state, "God will care for and provide for those He calls. Sometimes He provides a salary. Sometimes He provides a job that we can do to supplement our income." In what ways have you seen God provide for your needs?

   Was it in the way you expected?

6. On page 132, I write, "We hear a lot of teaching about prosperity, and some of it gives the impression that if we are not driving a Lexus or a BMW, something must be wrong with our faith. I believe that God prospers His

people, but the purpose is not to make us extravagant but to make us capable of ministry." What are some practical ways you can live redemptively?

What are some practical ways you can touch a person here or there and make a difference in that person's life?

7.   What new concepts have you discovered during this study?

What things have you believed but had never developed or heard discussed before?

8.   In what ways has this study:

   · Changed your view of the church?
   · Changed your view of God?
   · Changed your view of yourself?
   · Changed your view of your family?
   · Changed your view of your church family?
   · Changed your view of your community?
   · Changed your view of the place you work?

CHAPTER 9

Thoughts for Leading the Church as a Force

I wrote chapter 9 primarily with pastors and church leaders in mind. If you are a church leader in some capacity, the following questions will help evaluate your leadership style and its effects, with the goal of enabling you to become effective in leading the church as a force. (This is a good study for church staff and leadership to do together.)

1. What does the statement, "Church community is vital, but it must always be vehicular to our ministry in the non-believing community" (page 139) mean to you in your situation?

2. What is meant by the term "micromanaging"?

    Why does it kill efforts to become a church as a force?

3. Have you recognized any of the signs on the staff "death list" on pages 140-141 in your church? If so, which ones?

    What practical steps can you take today to correct this problem?

4. What is involved with communicating a "picture" to those whom you are leading?

    Why is it important for those working with us to "see" what we are doing?

    How does this release creativity?

5. What is meant by "choosing the wrong arrow"?

    Why is it considered a sure-fire murderer of the church as a force?

    Are there any "wrong arrows" in your church programs?

6. What are the two questions on page 144 for the church as a force to answer?

    How would you apply these questions to your congregation?

    Do you have reporting or evaluative mechanisms in place to accurately answer these questions?

7. On pages 146-152, I underscore four essential things that must be true in all our church life if we are to effectively release Jesus through the people we lead. What are these four things?

    How would you evaluate your own leadership in regard to each?

    How would the people who work under you evaluate your leadership in regard to each? (If you are brave, have those you work with do this evaluation with you.)

8. What is a "natural network" (see pages 148-150)?

    How can you discover these types of networks?

    How can you incorporate this concept into your current church life?

9. It is my belief that change takes place from the inside out. To do this, you must first identify a healthy core (see pages 153-154). Who would you consider your healthy core to be in your church?

Do your staff members (whether either paid or volunteer) have a healthy core that they are also developing?

How can you keep the core expanding and continuing to be healthy?

10. I also believe that telling stories is a key element in keeping the concept of the church as a force alive and well defined in the congregation (see pages 154-157). Do you have a forum for communicating your congregation's stories?

What are some ways this can be done? (One church has a monthly newspaper called *The Family Matters* that has a primary purpose of telling the church family stories.)

What are some church family stories that you can tell right now?

11. A final method to help you build your congregation into a church as a force is to communicate through interpreters (see pages 157-158). How would you describe this concept in your own words?

Who are your interpreters?

How can you be more intentional in developing this area of communication?

Acknowledgments

To update a 30-year-old book when I am 40 years older than it was a challenge. I cried "help!" . . . and put together a little team to help me.

I want to thank Dr. Amanda Pavich, Dr. Sundar Cook and Reverend Louis Locke Jr. These are tremendously talented leaders in their respective fields of archeology, psychology and pastoring. They took the time to read the original book and make invaluable suggestions that enabled me to see the concepts through much younger eyes.

My wife, Barbara, an accomplished author herself, read and improved each revision and rewrite. Thank you, Barb, for your loving partnership and encouragement not only in this project but also in our wonderful life together.

ABOUT THE AUTHORS

JERRY COOK is the author of *Love, Acceptance and Forgiveness* (written with Stanley Baldwin), the bestselling book that describes the church as a "healing force in the world." It was written during his pastorate at East Hill Church in Gresham, Oregon, and gives fresh encouragement and definition to churches, leaders and individuals of all denominations.

Jerry's second book, *A Few Things I've Learned Since I Knew it All* (also coauthored with Stanley Baldwin) brings new insights about God, ourselves, guidance, success, ministry and mystery. He has also written a book about marriage with his wife, Barbara, called *Choosing to Love*, and his latest book, *The Monday Morning Church: Out of the Sanctuary and into the Streets*, draws from the New Testament letter to the Ephesians and lays out how Christians can be the church not just in buildings on Sunday but also 24/7 in everyday living. Jerry was also a contributor to the *Spirit Filled Life Bible*, authoring the textual notes and outlines for the books of 1 Samuel, 2 Samuel and Joel.

In 1965, Jerry became the senior pastor of East Hill Church in Gresham, Oregon, (in the Portland metropolitan area). His perspective on the role of the church in the world helped the church expand from a handful of people to more than 4,500 in attendance. East Hill Church continues to be a growing and influential congregation.

After 19 years at East Hill Church, the Cooks moved to Kirkland, Washington (in the Seattle area), where Jerry was an associate pastor at Eastside Foursquare Church. He retired from that position in September of 2007. The Cooks now live on Whidbey Island, where Jerry maintains a teaching and church consulting ministry. He also addresses conventions and conferences throughout the United States and overseas.

Jerry is a graduate of Seattle Pacific University (BA) and Fuller Theological Seminary (M.Div.) He also holds Doctor of Divinity degrees from Life Pacific College in Los Angeles, California, as well as Pacific Life College in Canada. He and his wife, Barbara, are the recipients of the Medallion Award from Seattle Pacific University in tribute to their accomplishments as a professional team.

When Jerry is not teaching or traveling, you will find him fly-fishing on his favorite river, stream or mountain lake. He and Barbara have a family of four children (two boys and two girls) and five grandchildren.

To contact Jerry for speaking engagements and purchase books and audio materials, visit **www.jerrycook.org**.

STANLEY C. BALDWIN is an author and speaker based in the Pacific Northwest area. A former periodical editor and book editor, he has authored and coauthored 20 books, including four titles that have sold more than 250,000 copies each: *The Kink and I, Your Money Matters, What Did Jesus Say About That?* and *Love, Acceptance and Forgiveness*. Stanley's books have been translated into 11 languages, and he has lectured abroad in Nigeria, India, Japan, Singapore, Taiwan, the Philippines and Australia.

DISCOVER THE LOVING SIDE OF CONFLICT

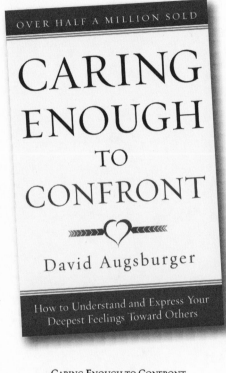

CARING ENOUGH TO CONFRONT
David Augsburger
ISBN 978.08307.46491
ISBN 08307.46498

Many people try to avoid conflict, but confrontation can be a catalyst for deeper loving care as we learn to integrate our needs and wants with those of others. Dr. David Augsburger believes that deepened relationships bloom out of conflict when we remember that the important issue is not what the conflict is about but instead how the conflict is handled. *Caring Enough to Confront* will teach you how to build trust, cope with blame and prejudice, and be honest about anger and frustration. You'll learn how to confront with compassion in family, church and work relationships to resolve conflict in a healthy and healing way. Make the most out of every conflict by mastering the tools of making peace.